ANNE
FRANK

BY DIEGO AGRIMBAU   ILLUSTRATED BY FABIÁN MEZQUITA

CAPSTONE PRESS
a capstone imprint

Graphic Library is published by Capstone Press,
1710 Roe Crest Drive, North Mankato, Minnesota 56003
www.mycapstone.com

Cataloging-in-Publication Data is available at the Library of
Congress website.
ISBN 978-1-5157-9161-4 (library binding)
ISBN 978-1-5157-9165-2 (paperback)
ISBN 978-1-5157-9169-0 (eBook PDF)

Summary: A graphic novel retelling of *The Diary of a
Young Girl*.

Author: Diego Agrimbau
Illustrator: Fabián Mezquita

Translated into the English language by Trusted Translations

Printed in the United States of America.
010370F17

TABLE OF CONTENTS

Introducing

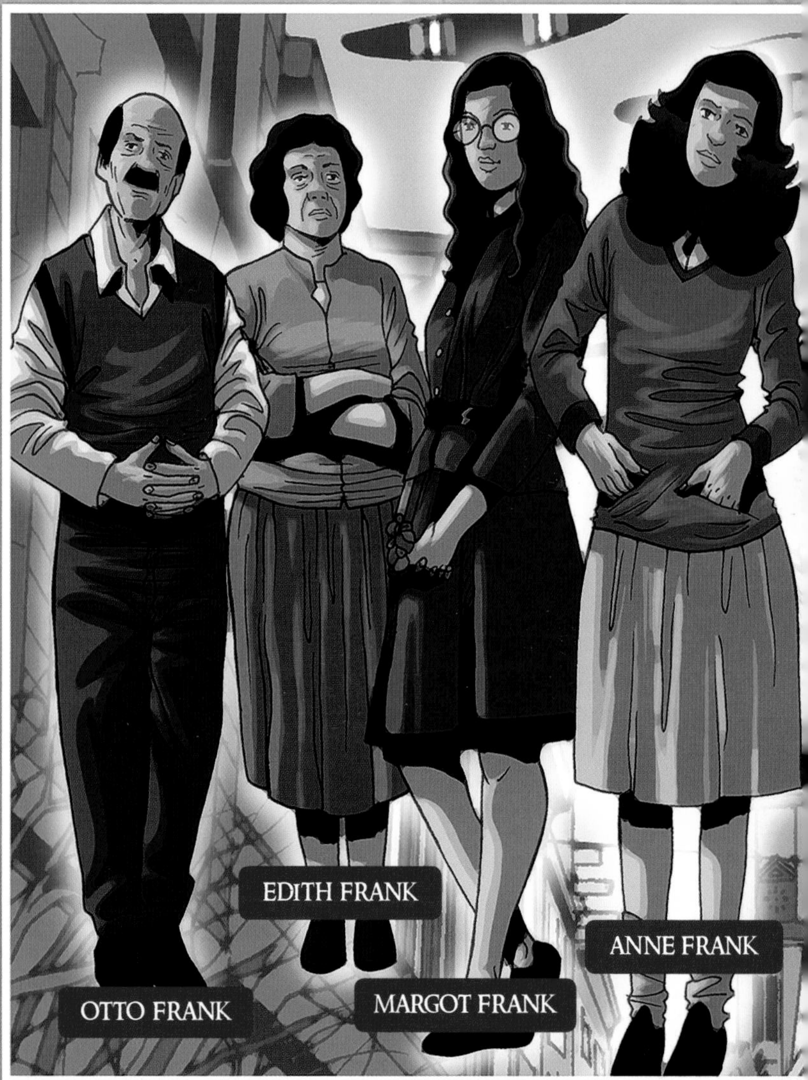
EDITH FRANK
ANNE FRANK
OTTO FRANK
MARGOT FRANK

MR. DUSSEL

MRS. VAN DAAN

PETER VAN DAAN

MR. VAN DAAN

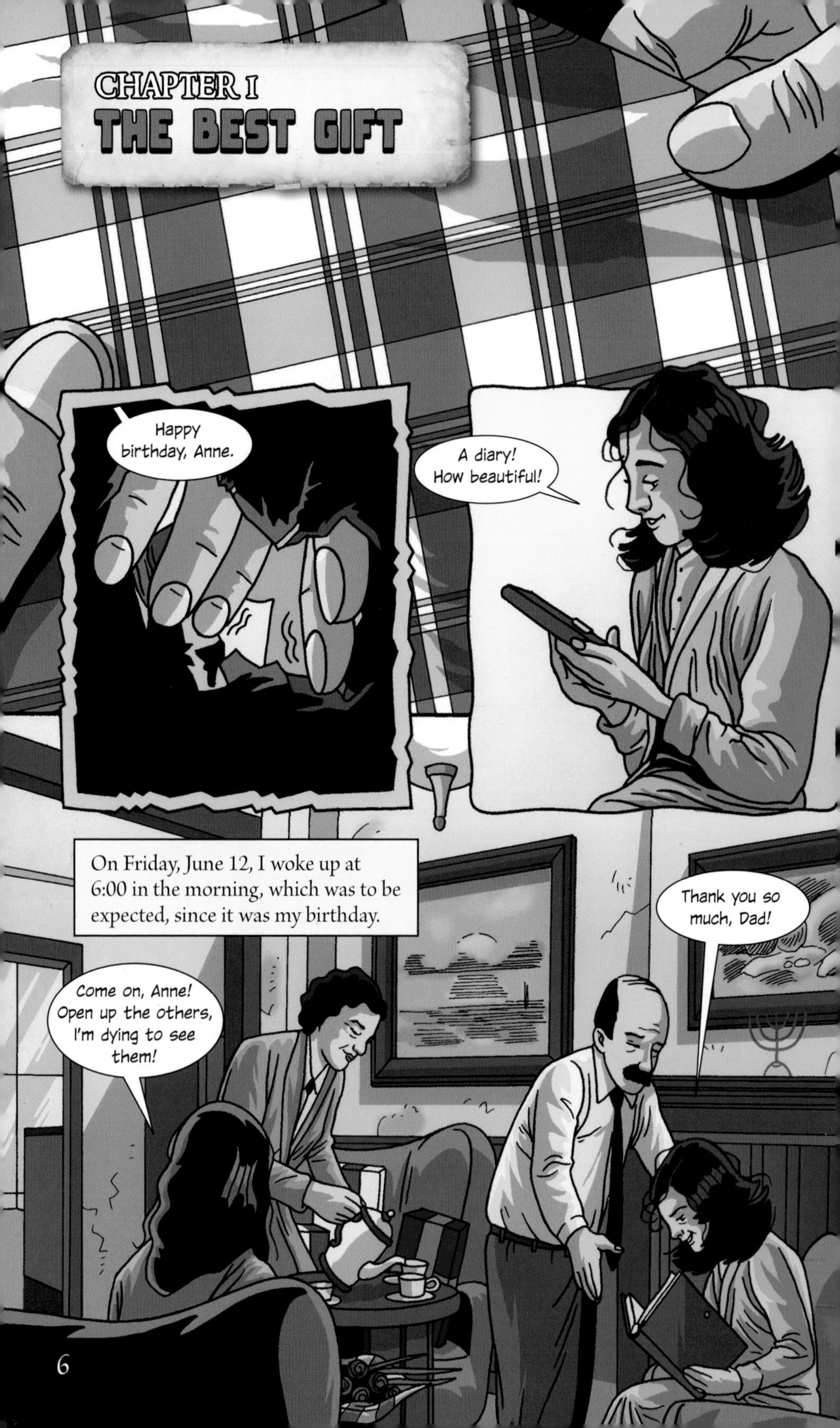
CHAPTER I
THE BEST GIFT
Happy birthday, Anne.
A diary! How beautiful!
On Friday, June 12, I woke up at 6:00 in the morning, which was to be expected, since it was my birthday.
Thank you so much, Dad!
Come on, Anne! Open up the others, I'm dying to see them!

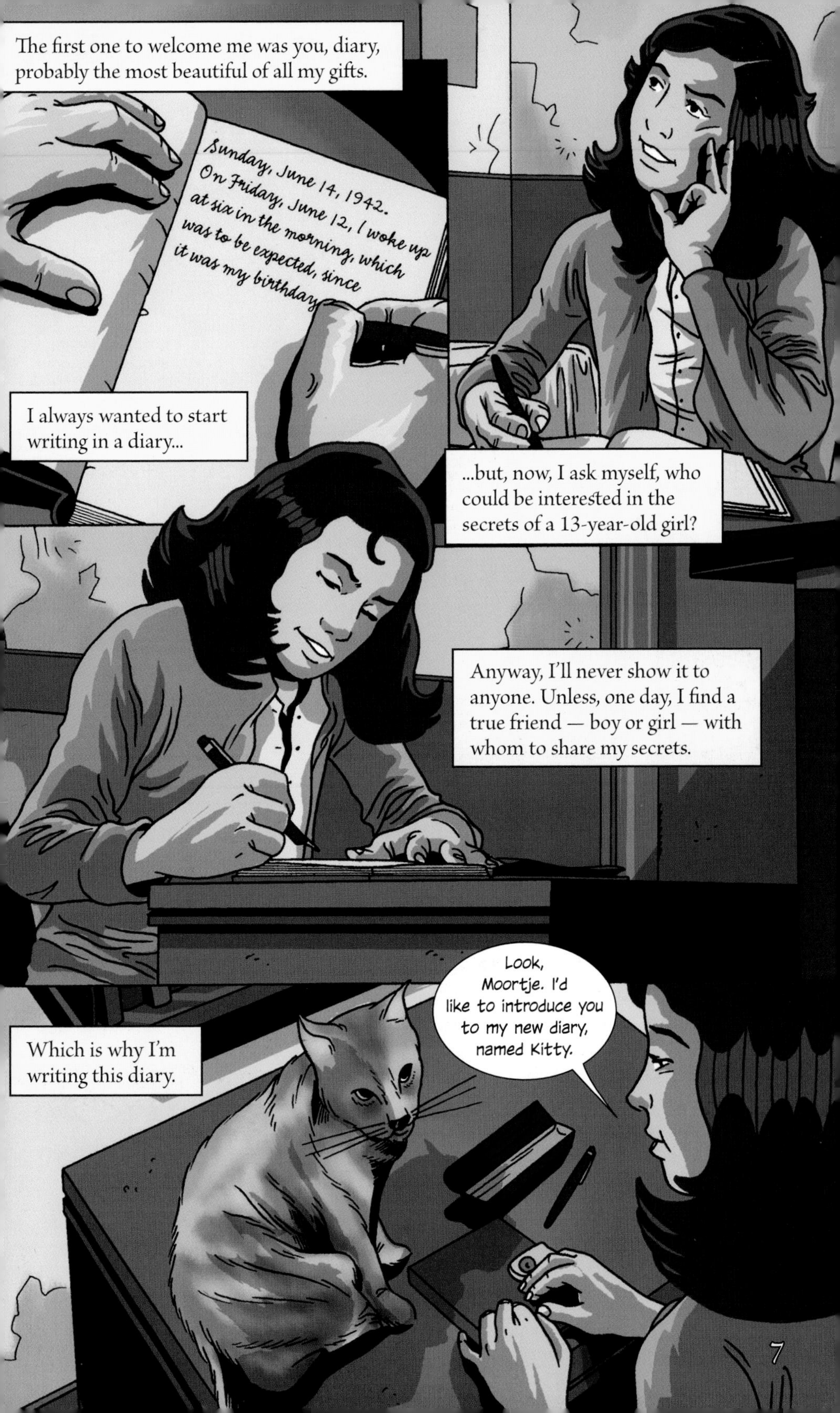

The first one to welcome me was you, diary, probably the most beautiful of all my gifts.
Sunday, June 14, 1942.
On Friday, June 12, I woke up at six in the morning, which was to be expected, since it was my birthday
I always wanted to start writing in a diary...
...but, now, I ask myself, who could be interested in the secrets of a 13-year-old girl?
Anyway, I'll never show it to anyone. Unless, one day, I find a true friend — boy or girl — with whom to share my secrets.
Which is why I'm writing this diary.
Look, Moortje. I'd like to introduce you to my new diary, named Kitty.

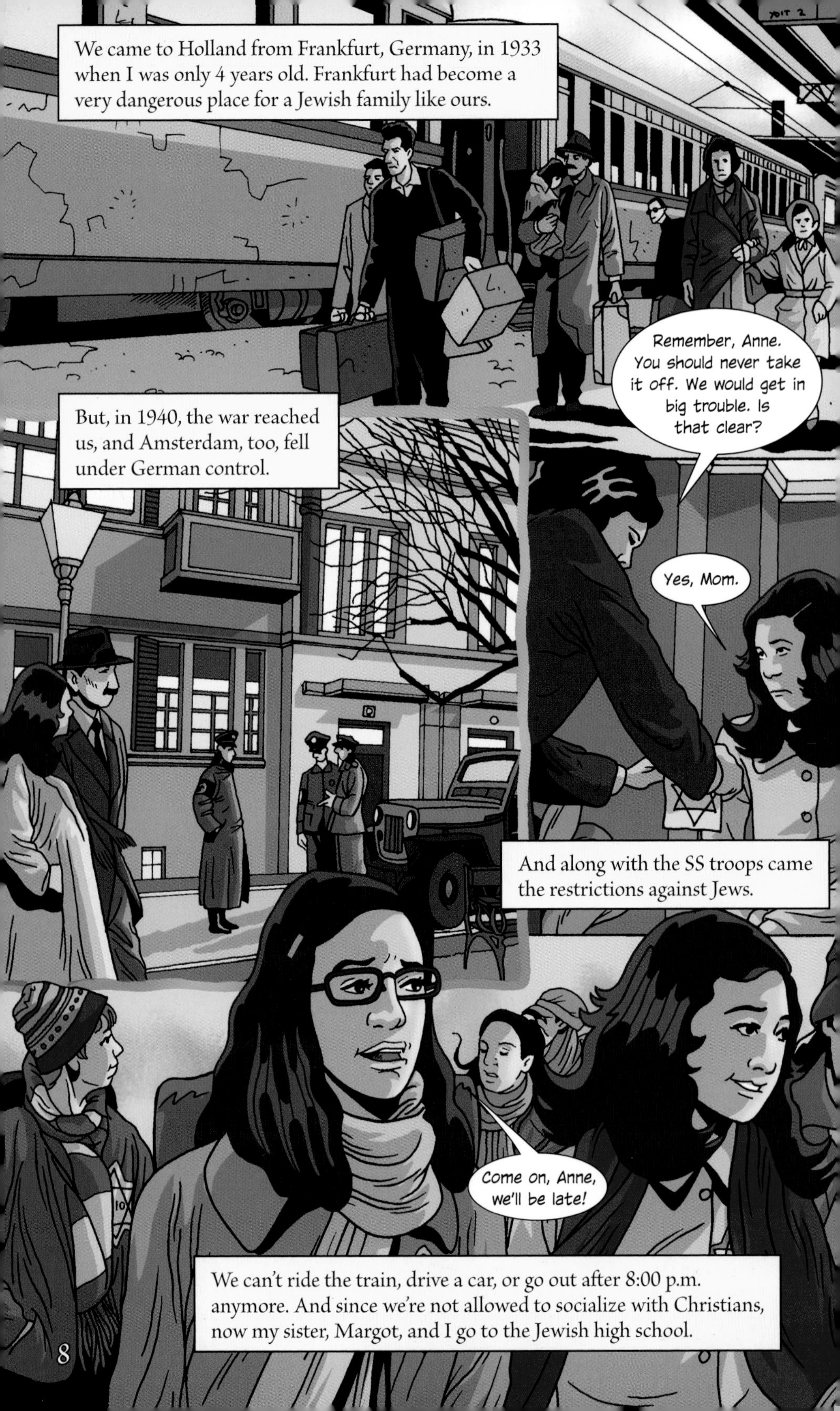
We came to Holland from Frankfurt, Germany, in 1933 when I was only 4 years old. Frankfurt had become a very dangerous place for a Jewish family like ours.
But, in 1940, the war reached us, and Amsterdam, too, fell under German control.
Remember, Anne. You should never take it off. We would get in big trouble. Is that clear?
Yes, Mom.
And along with the SS troops came the restrictions against Jews.
Come on, Anne, we'll be late!
We can't ride the train, drive a car, or go out after 8:00 p.m. anymore. And since we're not allowed to socialize with Christians, now my sister, Margot, and I go to the Jewish high school.

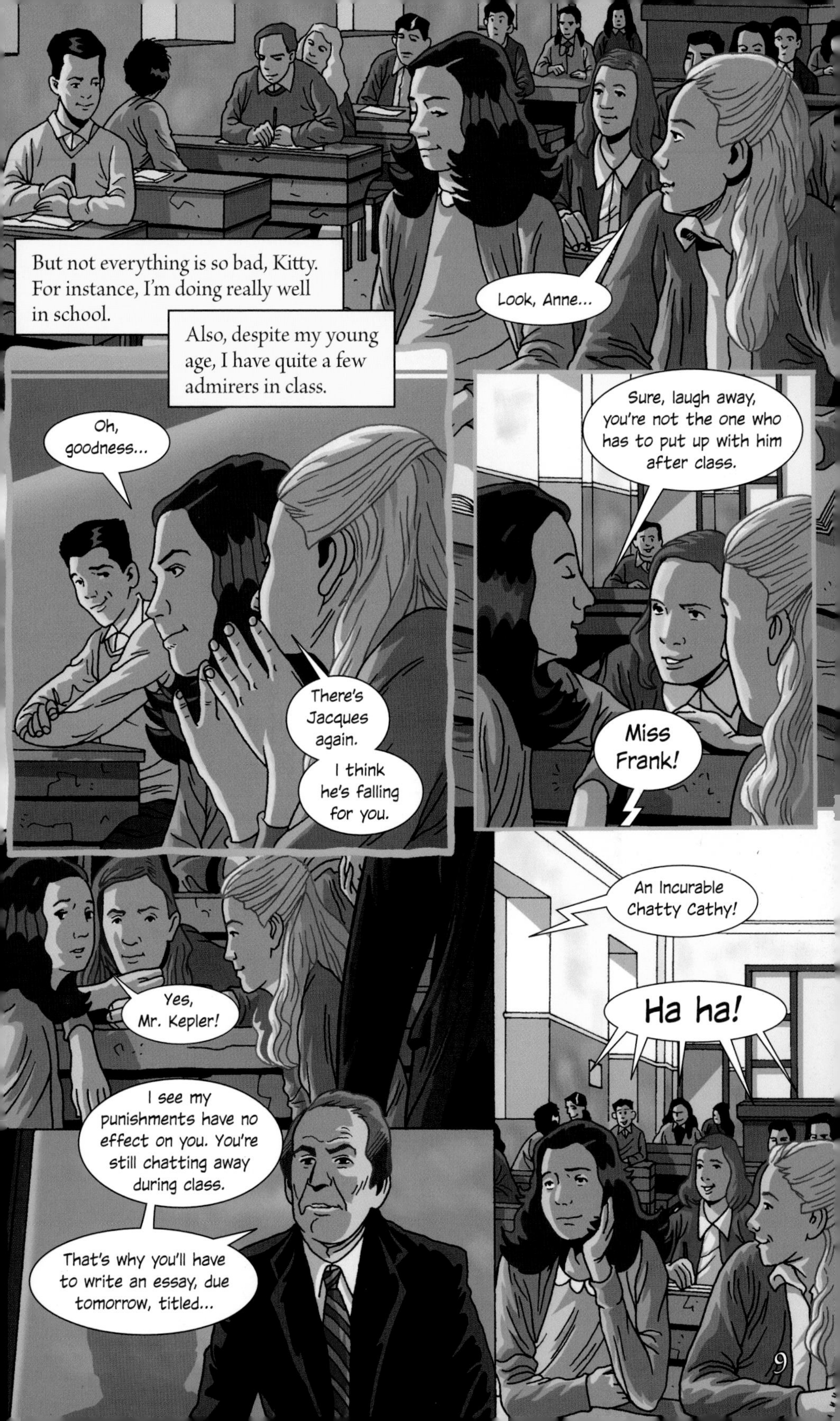

But not everything is so bad, Kitty. For instance, I'm doing really well in school.
Also, despite my young age, I have quite a few admirers in class.
Look, Anne...
Oh, goodness...
There's Jacques again.
I think he's falling for you.
Sure, laugh away, you're not the one who has to put up with him after class.
Miss Frank!
Yes, Mr. Kepler!
I see my punishments have no effect on you. You're still chatting away during class.
That's why you'll have to write an essay, due tomorrow, titled...
An Incurable Chatty Cathy!
Ha ha!

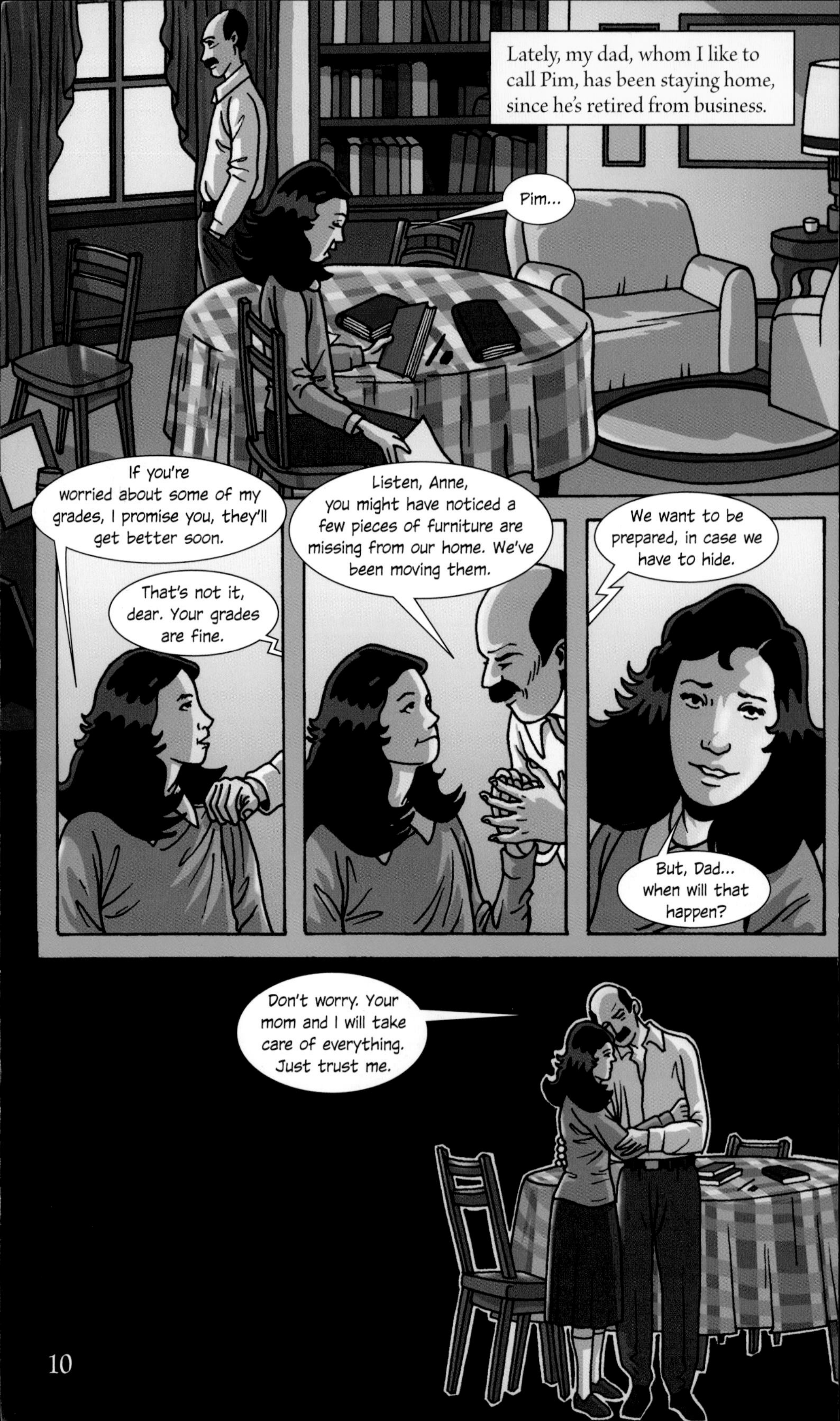

Lately, my dad, whom I like to call Pim, has been staying home, since he's retired from business.
Pim...
If you're worried about some of my grades, I promise you, they'll get better soon.
That's not it, dear. Your grades are fine.
Listen, Anne, you might have noticed a few pieces of furniture are missing from our home. We've been moving them.
We want to be prepared, in case we have to hide.
But, Dad... when will that happen?
Don't worry. Your mom and I will take care of everything. Just trust me.

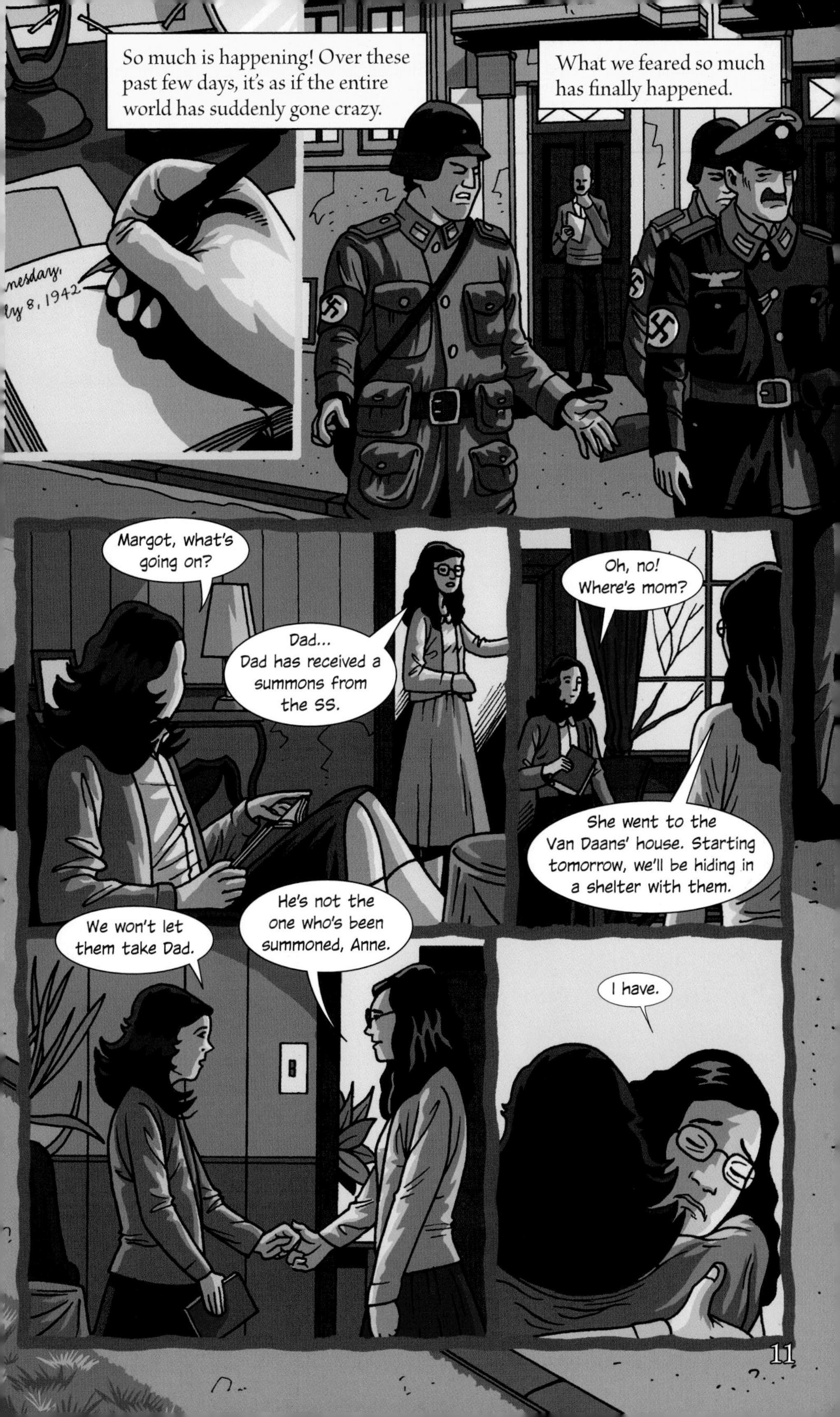

nesday,
ly 8, 1942
So much is happening! Over these past few days, it's as if the entire world has suddenly gone crazy.
What we feared so much has finally happened.
Margot, what's going on?
Dad... Dad has received a summons from the SS.
Oh, no! Where's mom?
She went to the Van Daans' house. Starting tomorrow, we'll be hiding in a shelter with them.
We won't let them take Dad.
He's not the one who's been summoned, Anne.
I have.

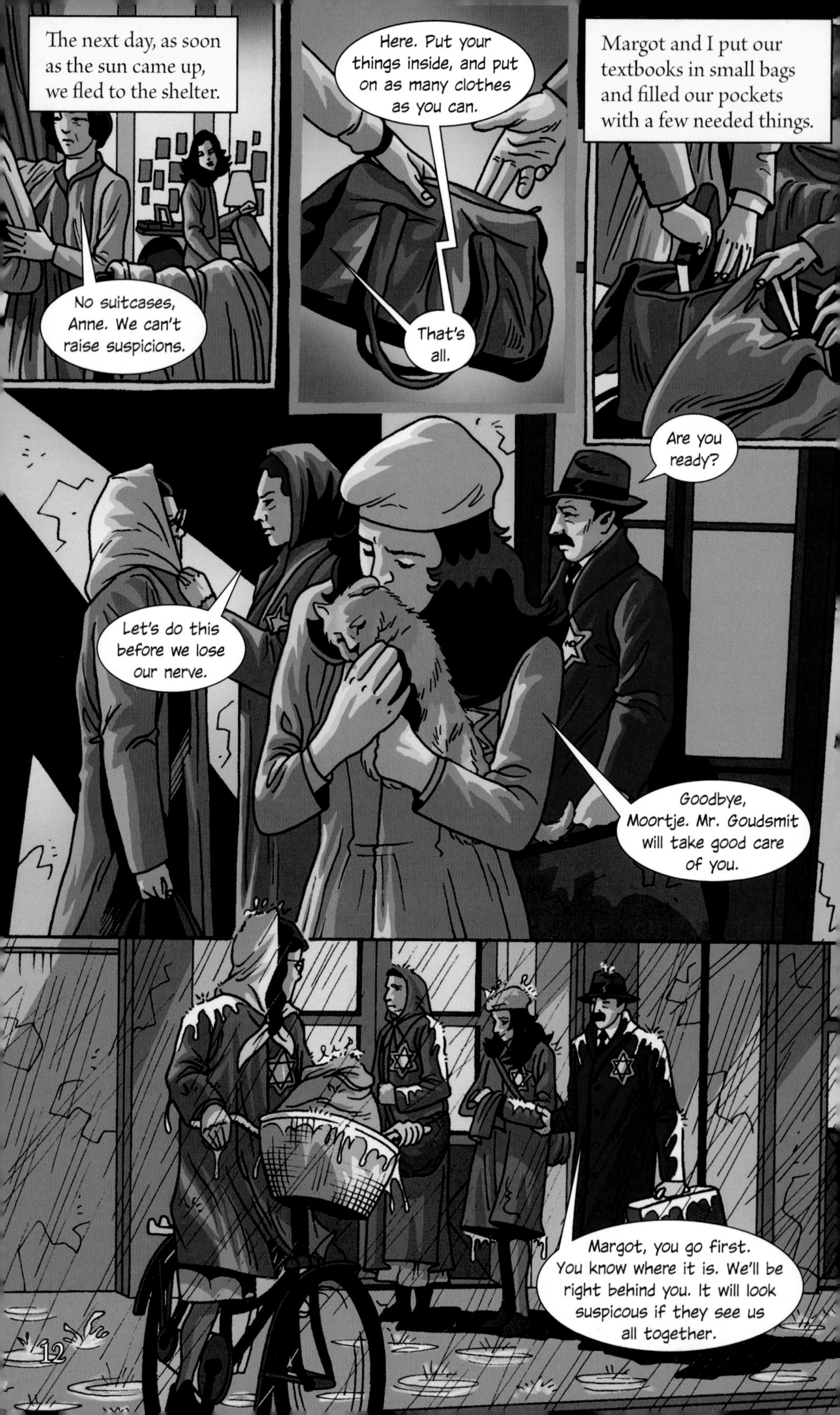

The next day, as soon as the sun came up, we fled to the shelter.
No suitcases, Anne. We can't raise suspicions.
Here. Put your things inside, and put on as many clothes as you can.
That's all.
Margot and I put our textbooks in small bags and filled our pockets with a few needed things.
Are you ready?
Let's do this before we lose our nerve.
Goodbye, Moortje. Mr. Goudsmit will take good care of you.
Margot, you go first. You know where it is. We'll be right behind you. It will look suspicous if they see us all together.

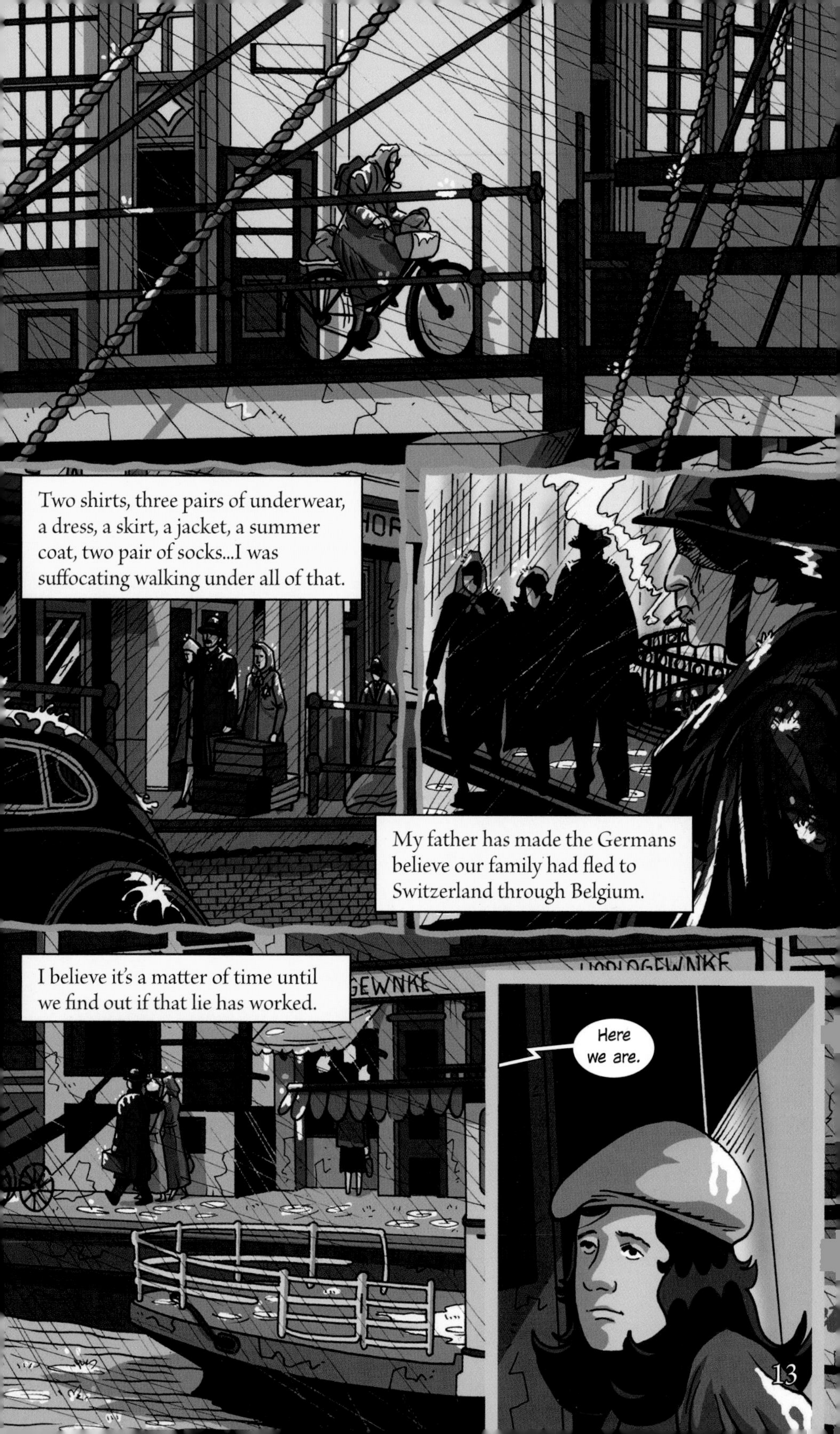
Two shirts, three pairs of underwear, a dress, a skirt, a jacket, a summer coat, two pair of socks...I was suffocating walking under all of that.
My father has made the Germans believe our family had fled to Switzerland through Belgium.
I believe it's a matter of time until we find out if that lie has worked.
Here we are.

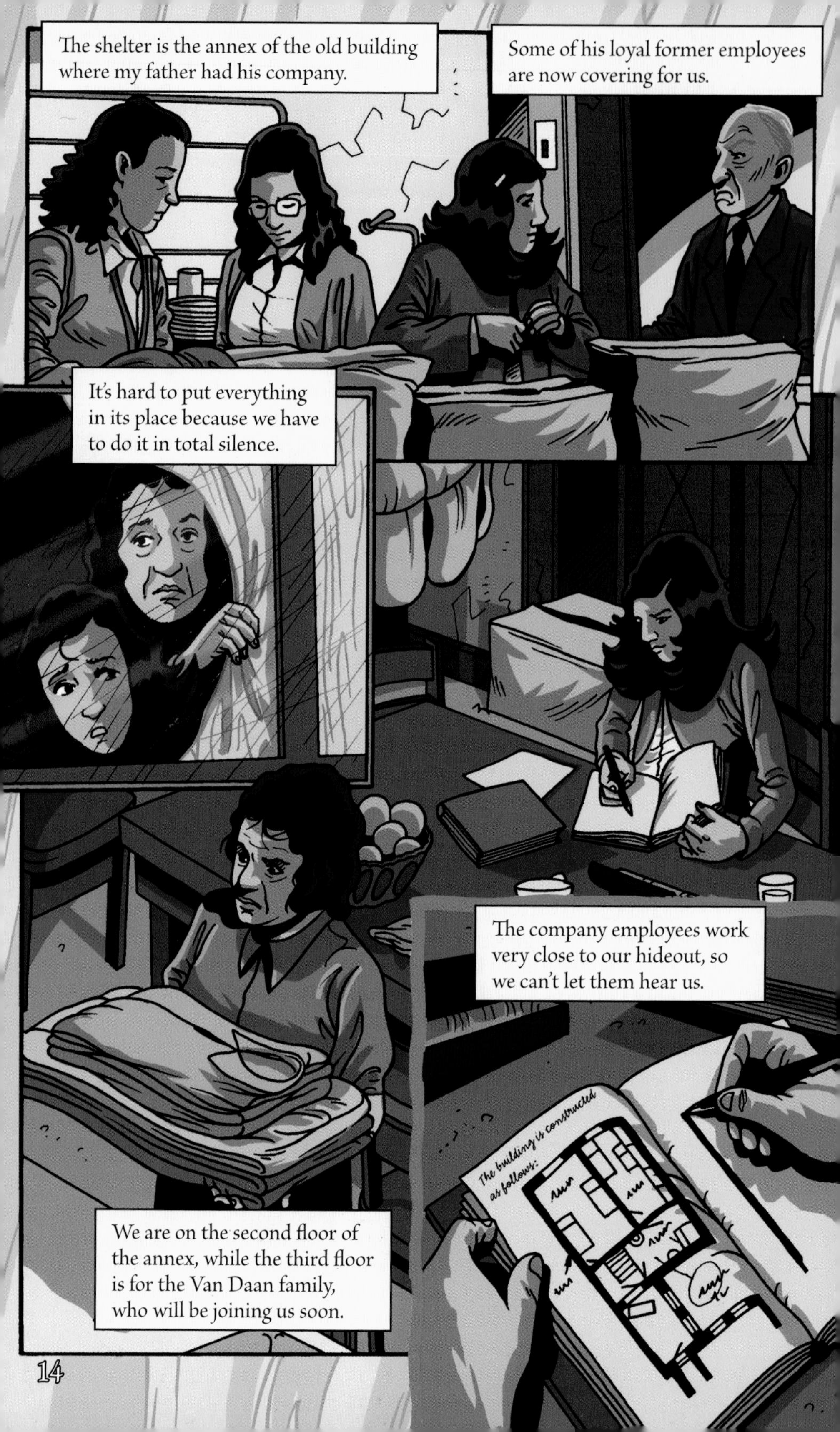
The shelter is the annex of the old building where my father had his company.
Some of his loyal former employees are now covering for us.
It's hard to put everything in its place because we have to do it in total silence.
The company employees work very close to our hideout, so we can't let them hear us.
We are on the second floor of the annex, while the third floor is for the Van Daan family, who will be joining us soon.
The building is constructed as follows:

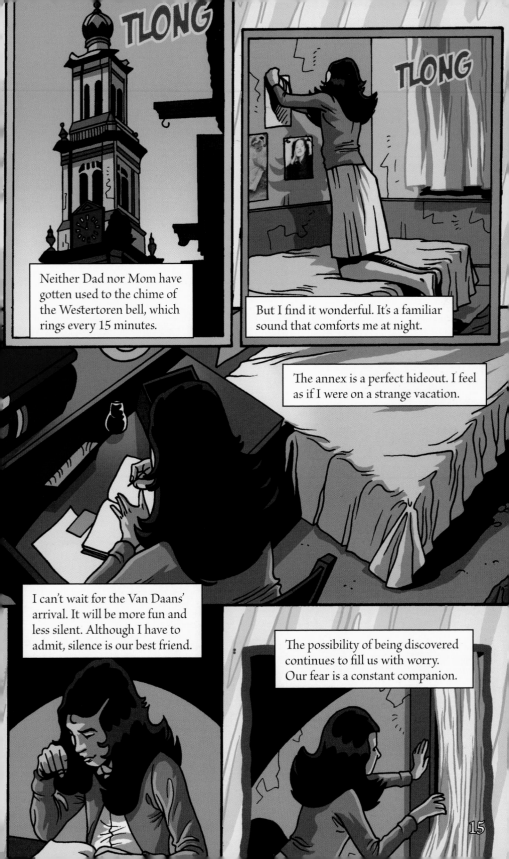

TLONG

TLONG

Neither Dad nor Mom have gotten used to the chime of the Westertoren bell, which rings every 15 minutes.

But I find it wonderful. It's a familiar sound that comforts me at night.

The annex is a perfect hideout. I feel as if I were on a strange vacation.

I can't wait for the Van Daans' arrival. It will be more fun and less silent. Although I have to admit, silence is our best friend.

The possibility of being discovered continues to fill us with worry. Our fear is a constant companion.

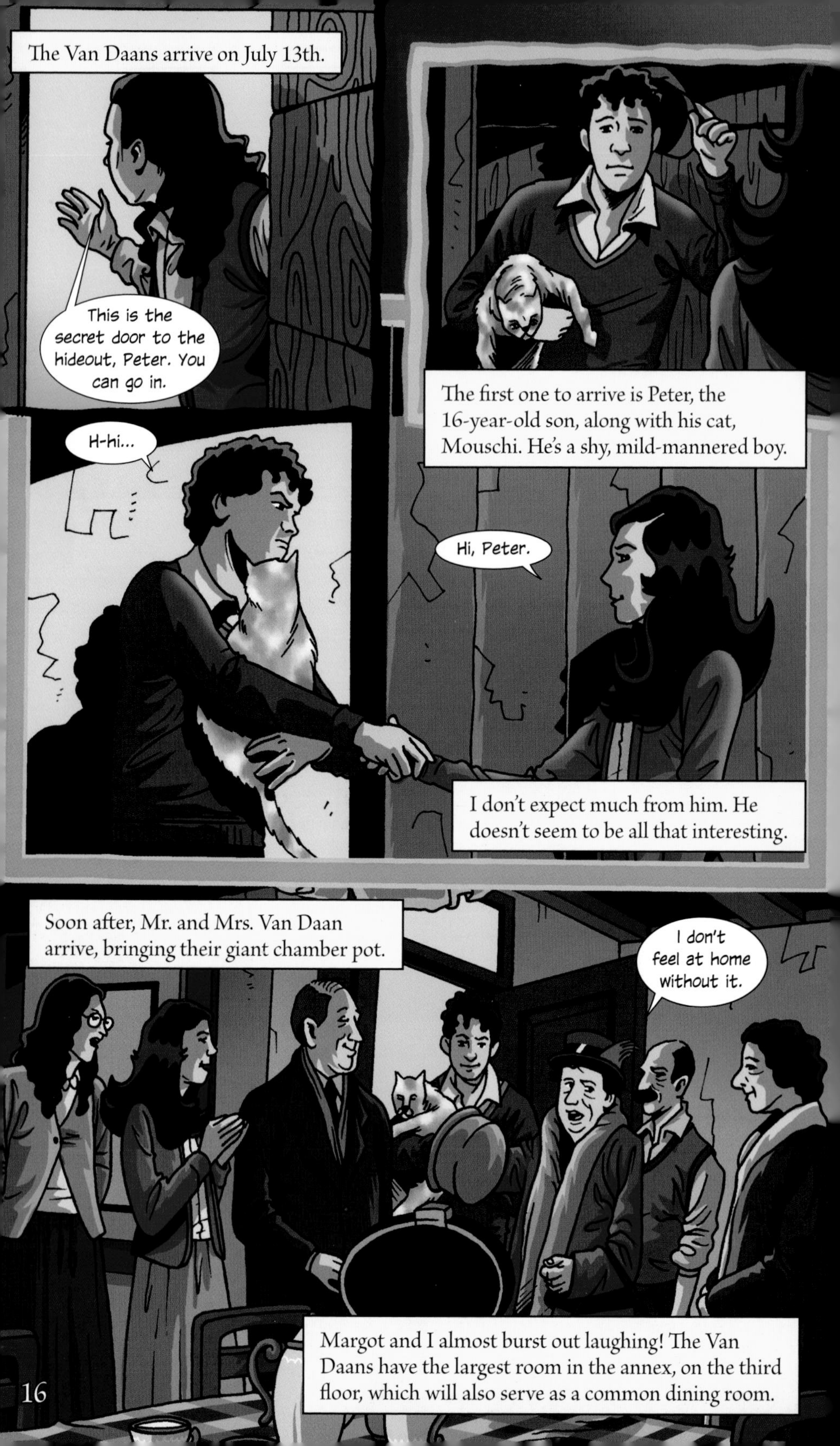

The Van Daans arrive on July 13th.
This is the secret door to the hideout, Peter. You can go in.
The first one to arrive is Peter, the 16-year-old son, along with his cat, Mouschi. He's a shy, mild-mannered boy.
H-hi...
Hi, Peter.
I don't expect much from him. He doesn't seem to be all that interesting.
Soon after, Mr. and Mrs. Van Daan arrive, bringing their giant chamber pot.
I don't feel at home without it.
Margot and I almost burst out laughing! The Van Daans have the largest room in the annex, on the third floor, which will also serve as a common dining room.

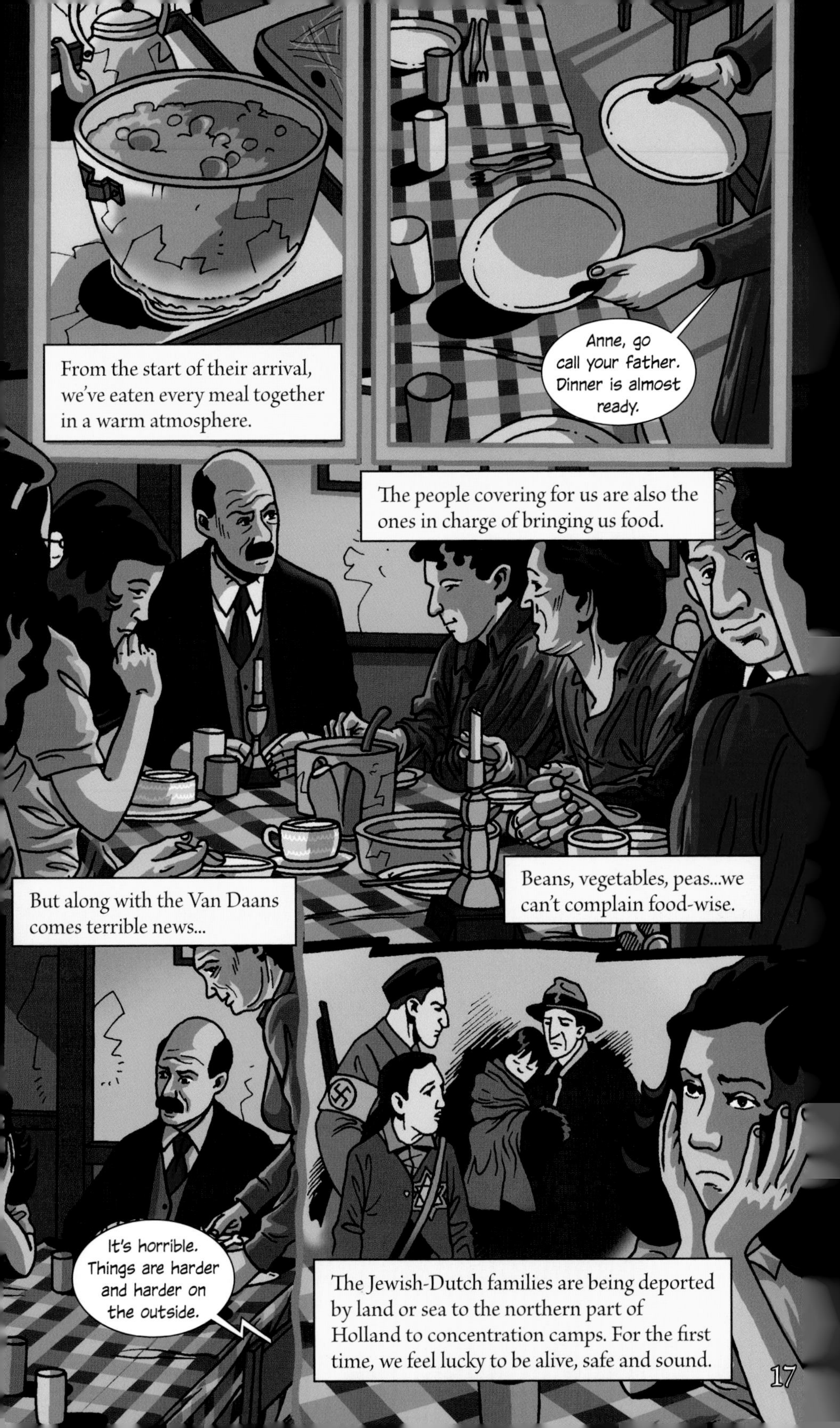
From the start of their arrival, we've eaten every meal together in a warm atmosphere.
Anne, go call your father. Dinner is almost ready.
The people covering for us are also the ones in charge of bringing us food.
But along with the Van Daans comes terrible news...
Beans, vegetables, peas...we can't complain food-wise.
It's horrible. Things are harder and harder on the outside.
The Jewish-Dutch families are being deported by land or sea to the northern part of Holland to concentration camps. For the first time, we feel lucky to be alive, safe and sound.

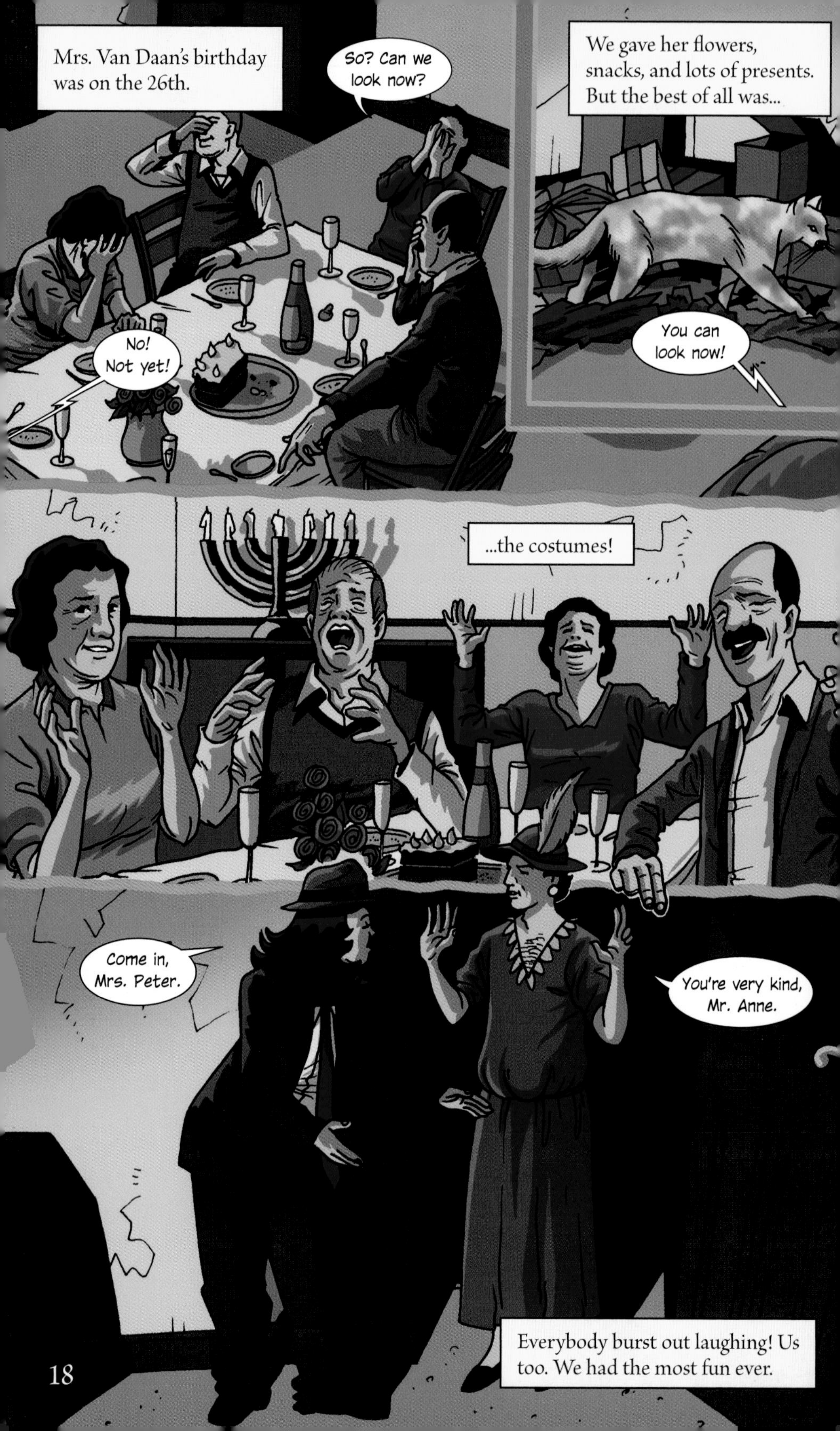

Mrs. Van Daan's birthday was on the 26th.
So? Can we look now?
No! Not yet!
We gave her flowers, snacks, and lots of presents. But the best of all was...
You can look now!
...the costumes!
Come in, Mrs. Peter.
You're very kind, Mr. Anne.
Everybody burst out laughing! Us too. We had the most fun ever.

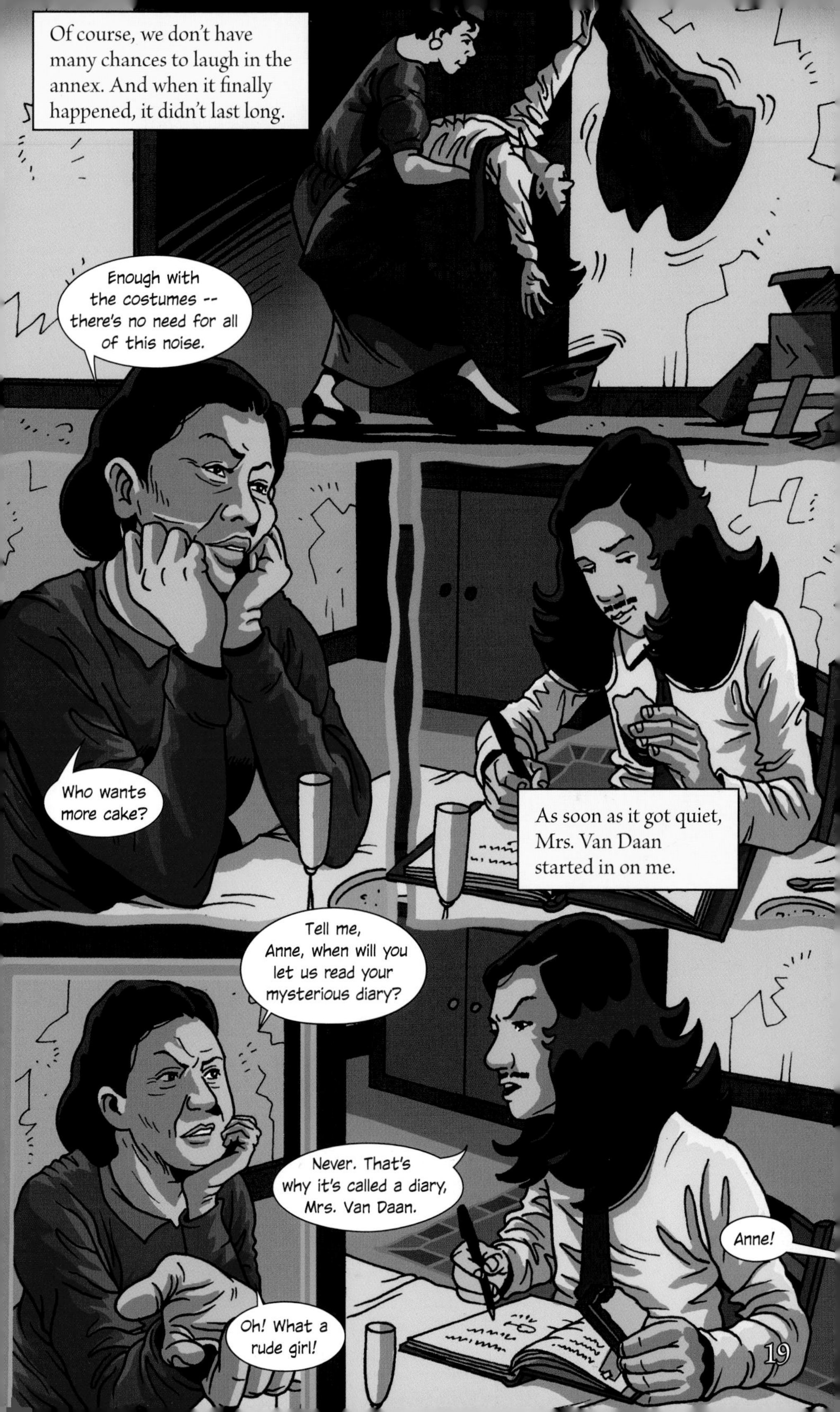

Of course, we don't have many chances to laugh in the annex. And when it finally happened, it didn't last long.
Enough with the costumes -- there's no need for all of this noise.
Who wants more cake?
As soon as it got quiet, Mrs. Van Daan started in on me.
Tell me, Anne, when will you let us read your mysterious diary?
Never. That's why it's called a diary, Mrs. Van Daan.
Anne!
Oh! What a rude girl!

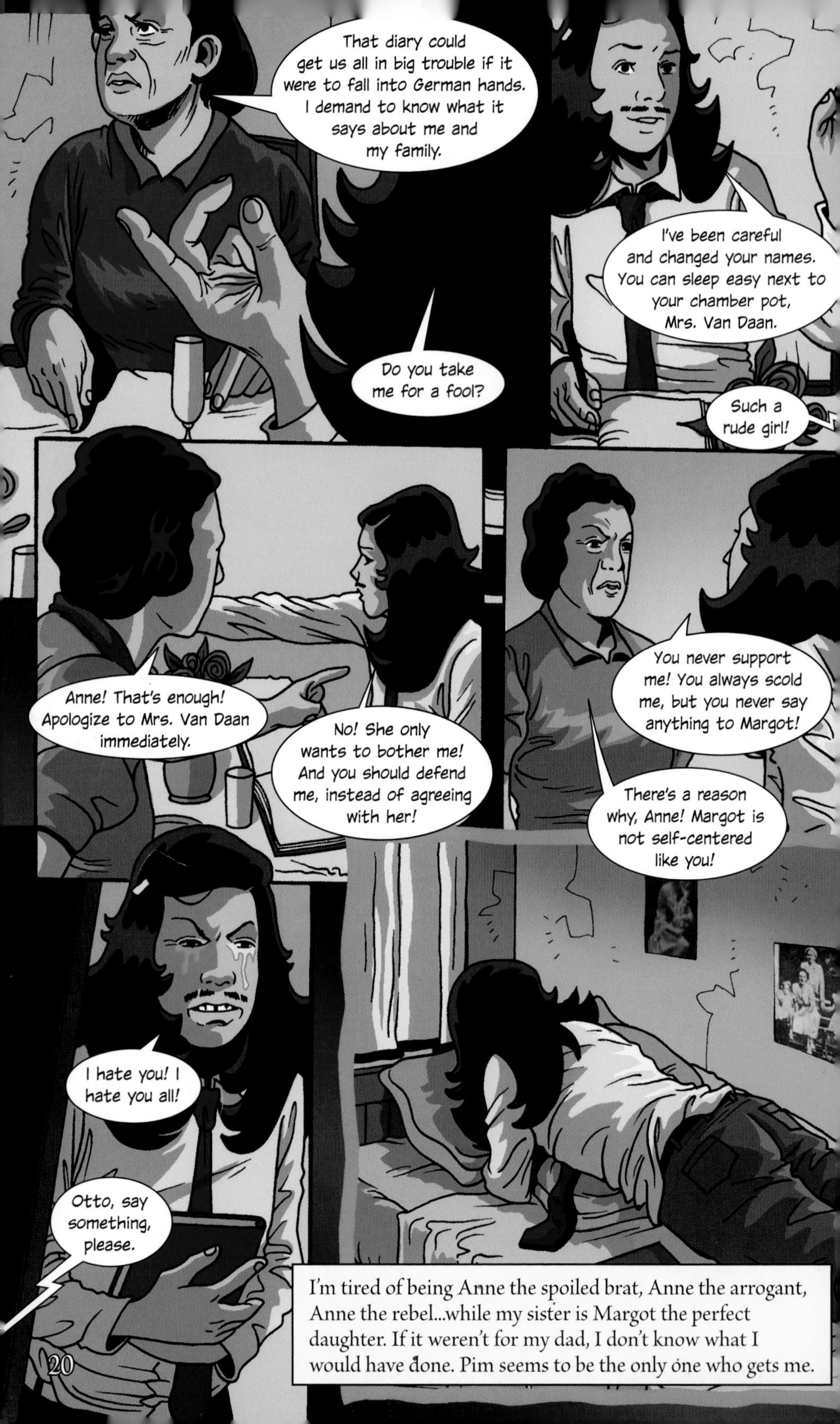

That diary could get us all in big trouble if it were to fall into German hands. I demand to know what it says about me and my family.
Do you take me for a fool?
I've been careful and changed your names. You can sleep easy next to your chamber pot, Mrs. Van Daan.
Such a rude girl!
Anne! That's enough! Apologize to Mrs. Van Daan immediately.
No! She only wants to bother me! And you should defend me, instead of agreeing with her!
You never support me! You always scold me, but you never say anything to Margot!
There's a reason why, Anne! Margot is not self-centered like you!
I hate you! I hate you all!
Otto, say something, please.
I'm tired of being Anne the spoiled brat, Anne the arrogant, Anne the rebel...while my sister is Margot the perfect daughter. If it weren't for my dad, I don't know what I would have done. Pim seems to be the only one who gets me.

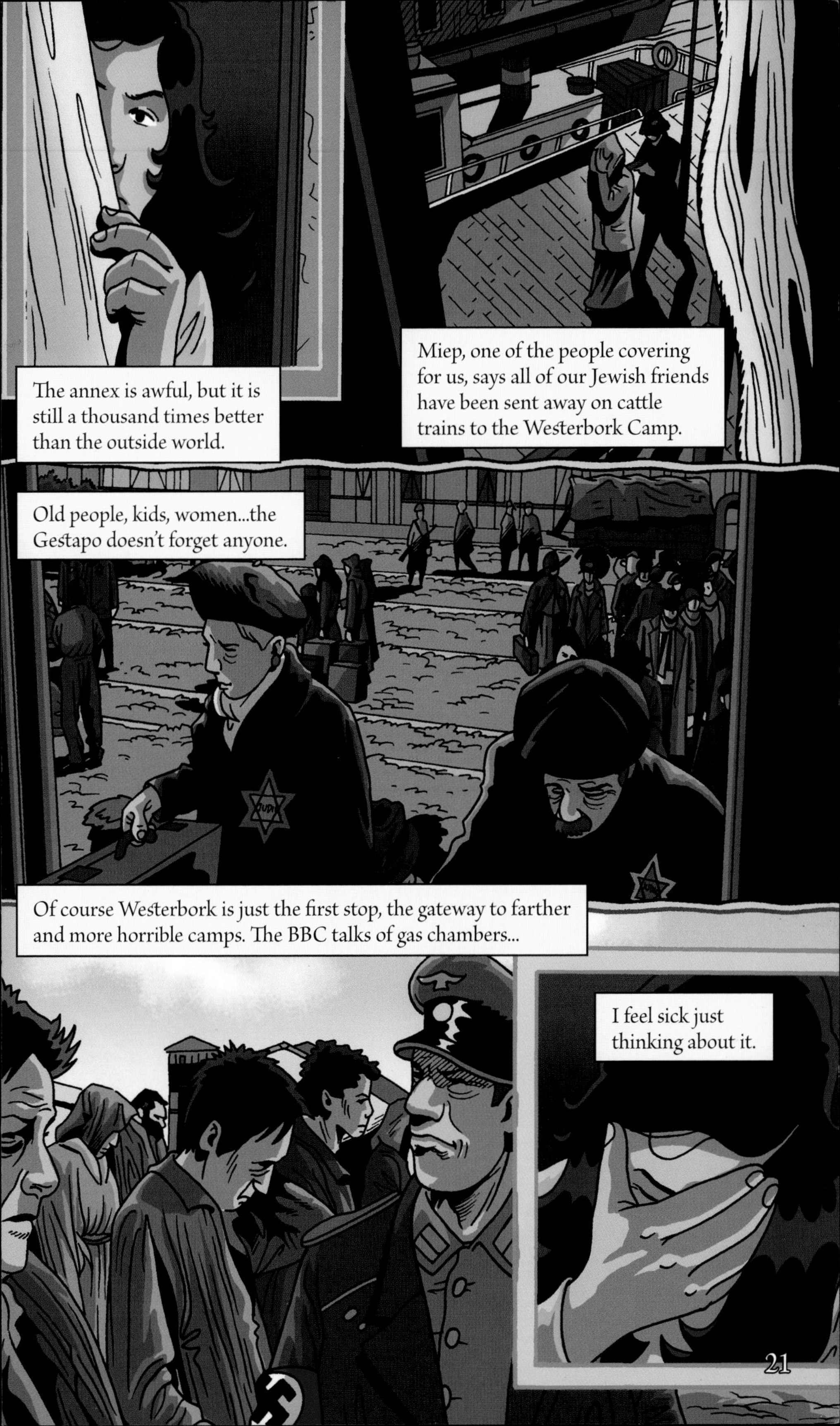
The annex is awful, but it is still a thousand times better than the outside world.
Miep, one of the people covering for us, says all of our Jewish friends have been sent away on cattle trains to the Westerbork Camp.
Old people, kids, women...the Gestapo doesn't forget anyone.
Of course Westerbork is just the first stop, the gateway to farther and more horrible camps. The BBC talks of gas chambers...
I feel sick just thinking about it.

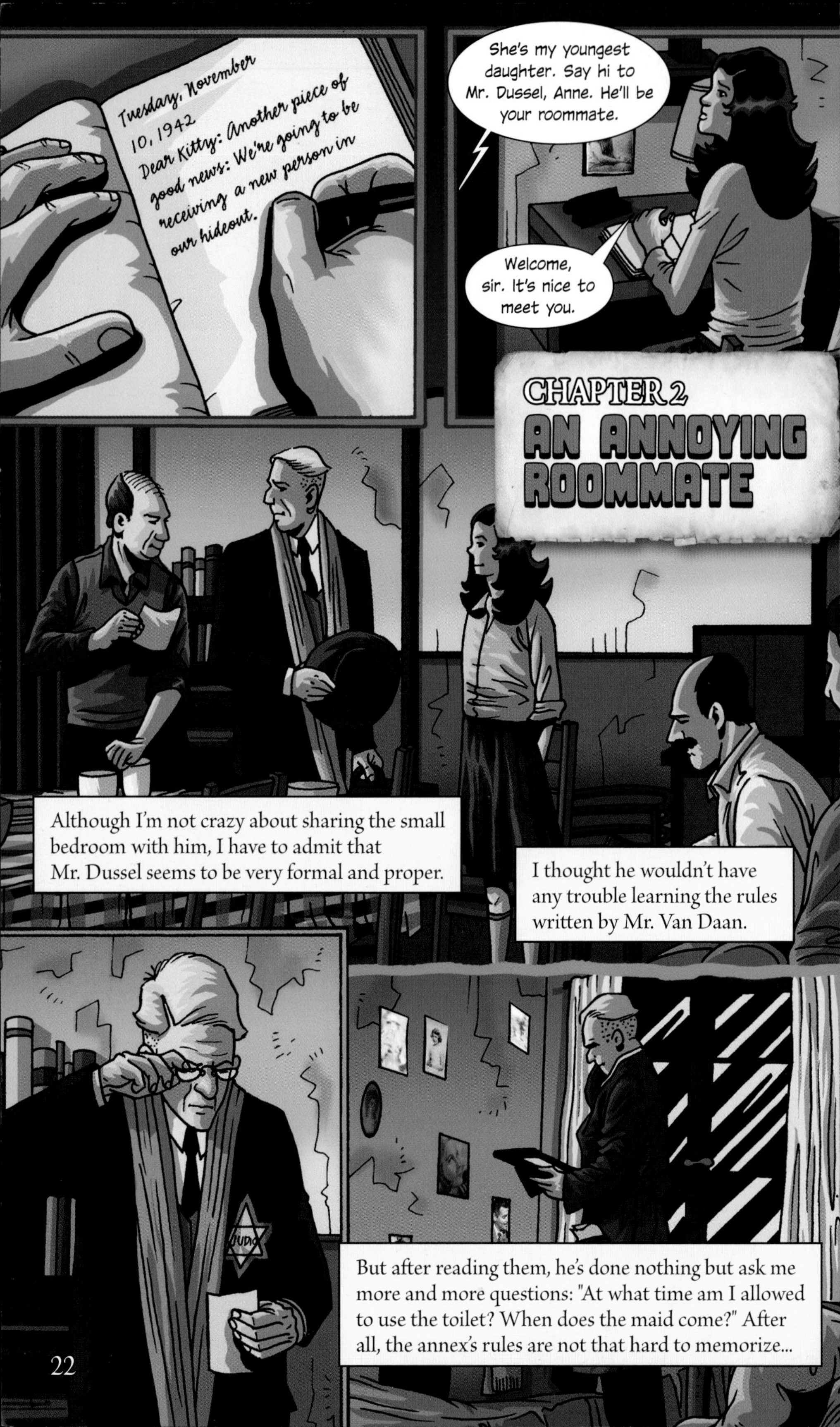
Tuesday, November 10, 1942
Dear Kitty: Another piece of good news: We're going to be receiving a new person in our hideout.
She's my youngest daughter. Say hi to Mr. Dussel, Anne. He'll be your roommate.
Welcome, sir. It's nice to meet you.
CHAPTER 2
AN ANNOYING ROOMMATE
Although I'm not crazy about sharing the small bedroom with him, I have to admit that Mr. Dussel seems to be very formal and proper.
I thought he wouldn't have any trouble learning the rules written by Mr. Van Daan.
JUDE
But after reading them, he's done nothing but ask me more and more questions: "At what time am I allowed to use the toilet? When does the maid come?" After all, the annex's rules are not that hard to memorize...

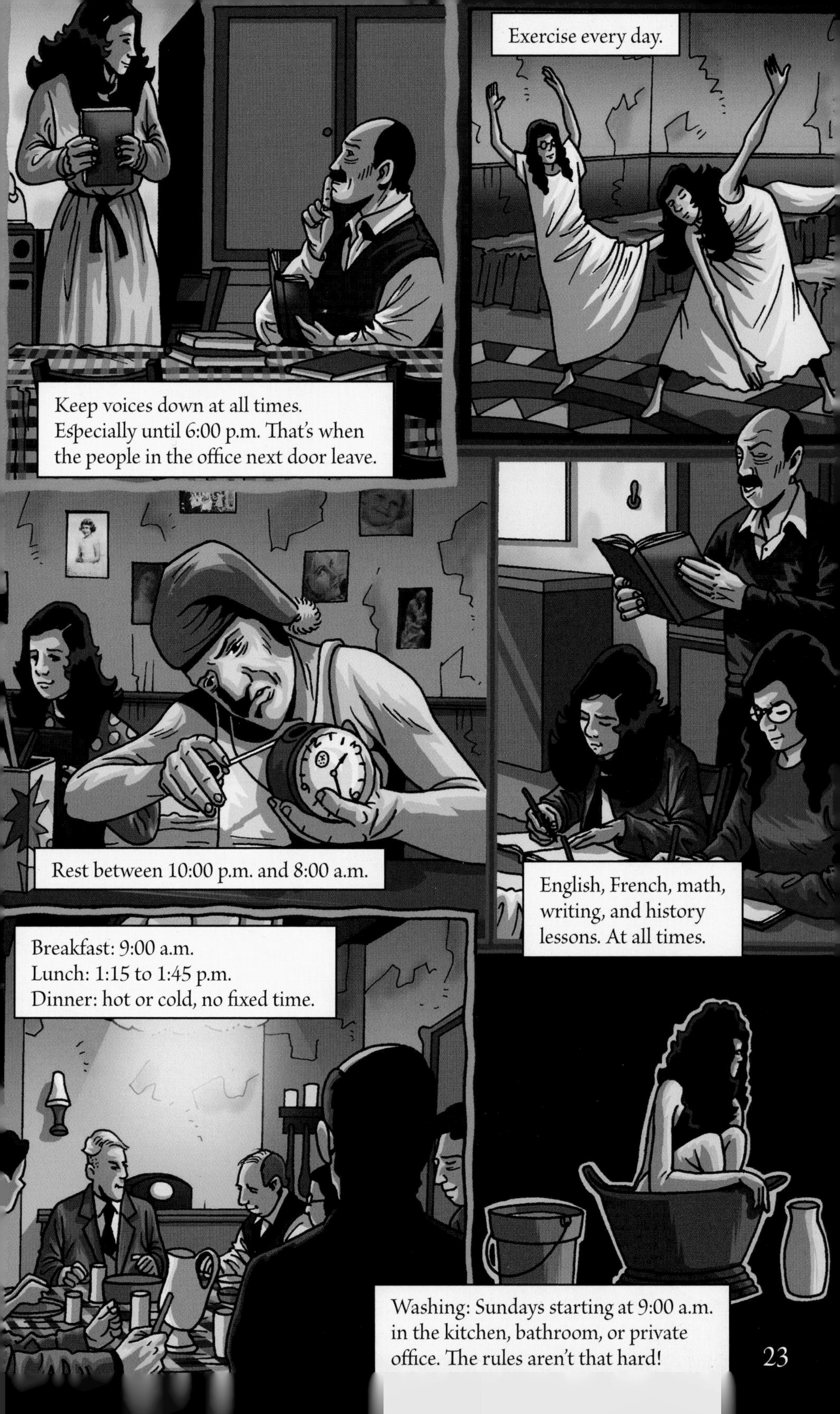
Keep voices down at all times. Especially until 6:00 p.m. That's when the people in the office next door leave.
Exercise every day.
Rest between 10:00 p.m. and 8:00 a.m.
English, French, math, writing, and history lessons. At all times.
Breakfast: 9:00 a.m.
Lunch: 1:15 to 1:45 p.m.
Dinner: hot or cold, no fixed time.
Washing: Sundays starting at 9:00 a.m. in the kitchen, bathroom, or private office. The rules aren't that hard!

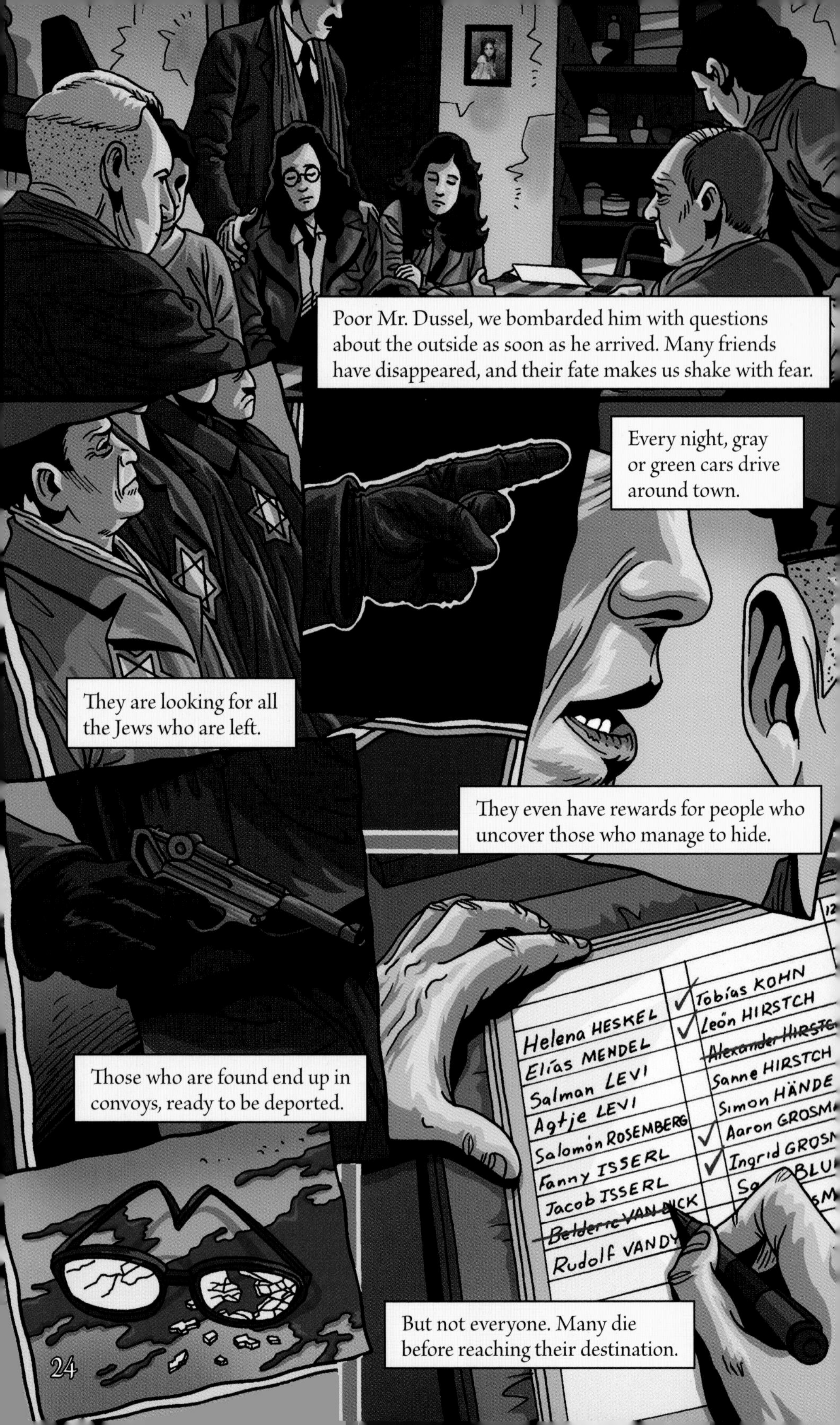
Poor Mr. Dussel, we bombarded him with questions about the outside as soon as he arrived. Many friends have disappeared, and their fate makes us shake with fear.
Every night, gray or green cars drive around town.
They are looking for all the Jews who are left.
They even have rewards for people who uncover those who manage to hide.
Helena HESKEL
Tobías KOHN
Elías MENDEL
León HIRSTCH
Salman LEVI
Sanne HIRSTCH
Agtje LEVI
Salomón ROSEMBERG
Fanny ISSERL
Jacob ISSERL
Those who are found end up in convoys, ready to be deported.
But not everyone. Many die before reaching their destination.

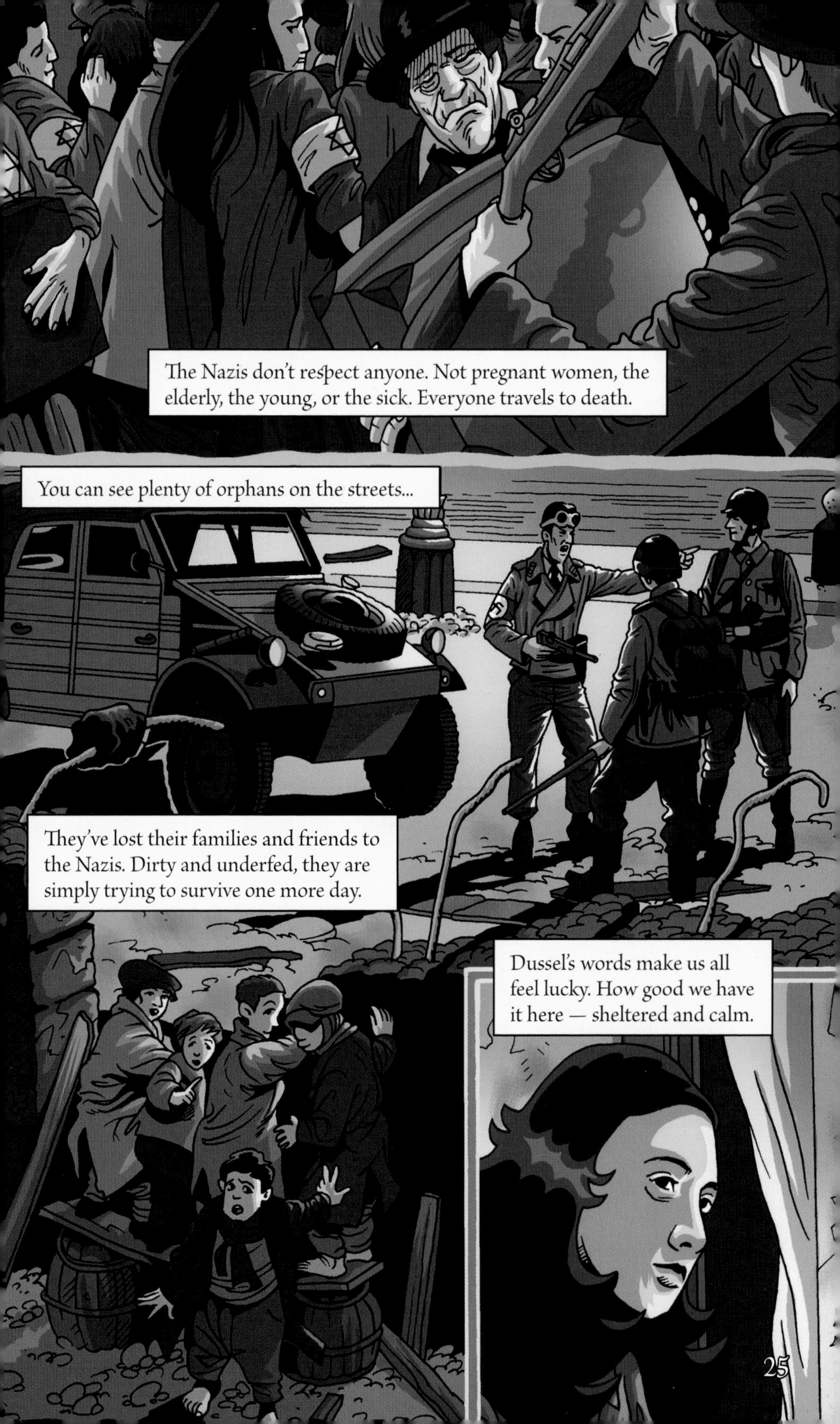
The Nazis don't respect anyone. Not pregnant women, the elderly, the young, or the sick. Everyone travels to death.
You can see plenty of orphans on the streets...
They've lost their families and friends to the Nazis. Dirty and underfed, they are simply trying to survive one more day.
Dussel's words make us all feel lucky. How good we have it here — sheltered and calm.

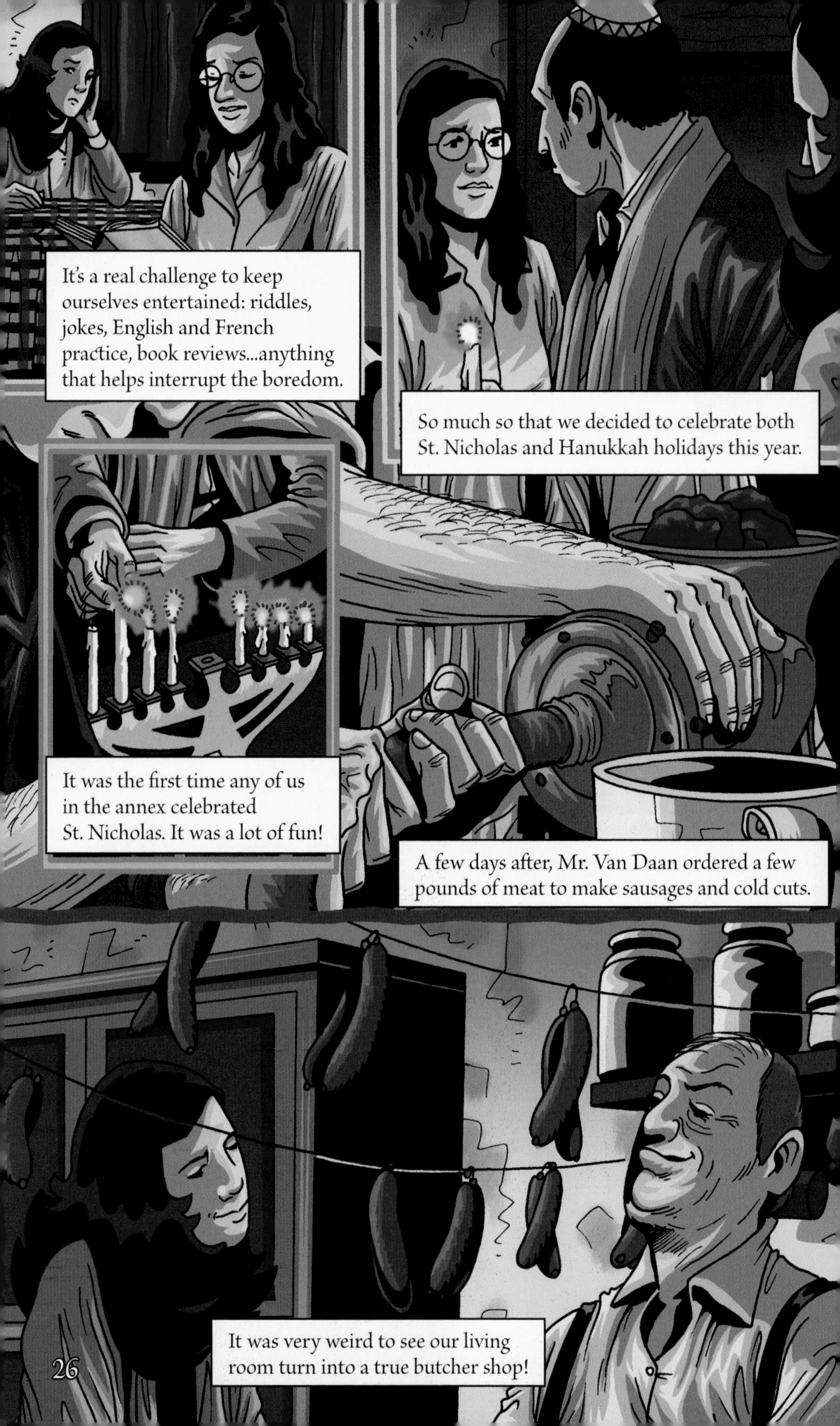
It's a real challenge to keep ourselves entertained: riddles, jokes, English and French practice, book reviews...anything that helps interrupt the boredom.
So much so that we decided to celebrate both St. Nicholas and Hanukkah holidays this year.
It was the first time any of us in the annex celebrated St. Nicholas. It was a lot of fun!
A few days after, Mr. Van Daan ordered a few pounds of meat to make sausages and cold cuts.
It was very weird to see our living room turn into a true butcher shop!

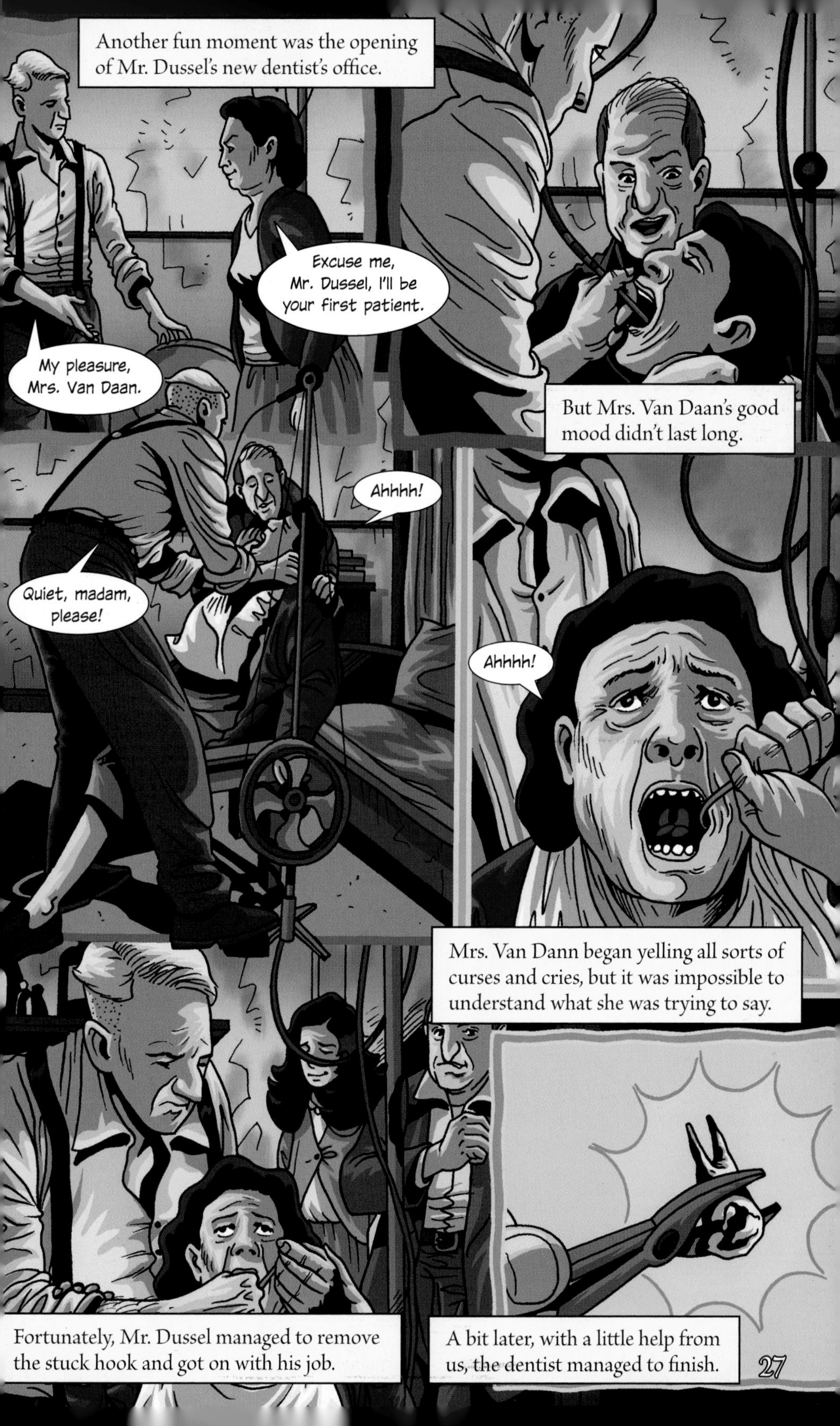
Another fun moment was the opening of Mr. Dussel's new dentist's office.
Excuse me, Mr. Dussel, I'll be your first patient.
My pleasure, Mrs. Van Daan.
But Mrs. Van Daan's good mood didn't last long.
Ahhhh!
Quiet, madam, please!
Ahhhh!
Mrs. Van Dann began yelling all sorts of curses and cries, but it was impossible to understand what she was trying to say.
Fortunately, Mr. Dussel managed to remove the stuck hook and got on with his job.
A bit later, with a little help from us, the dentist managed to finish.

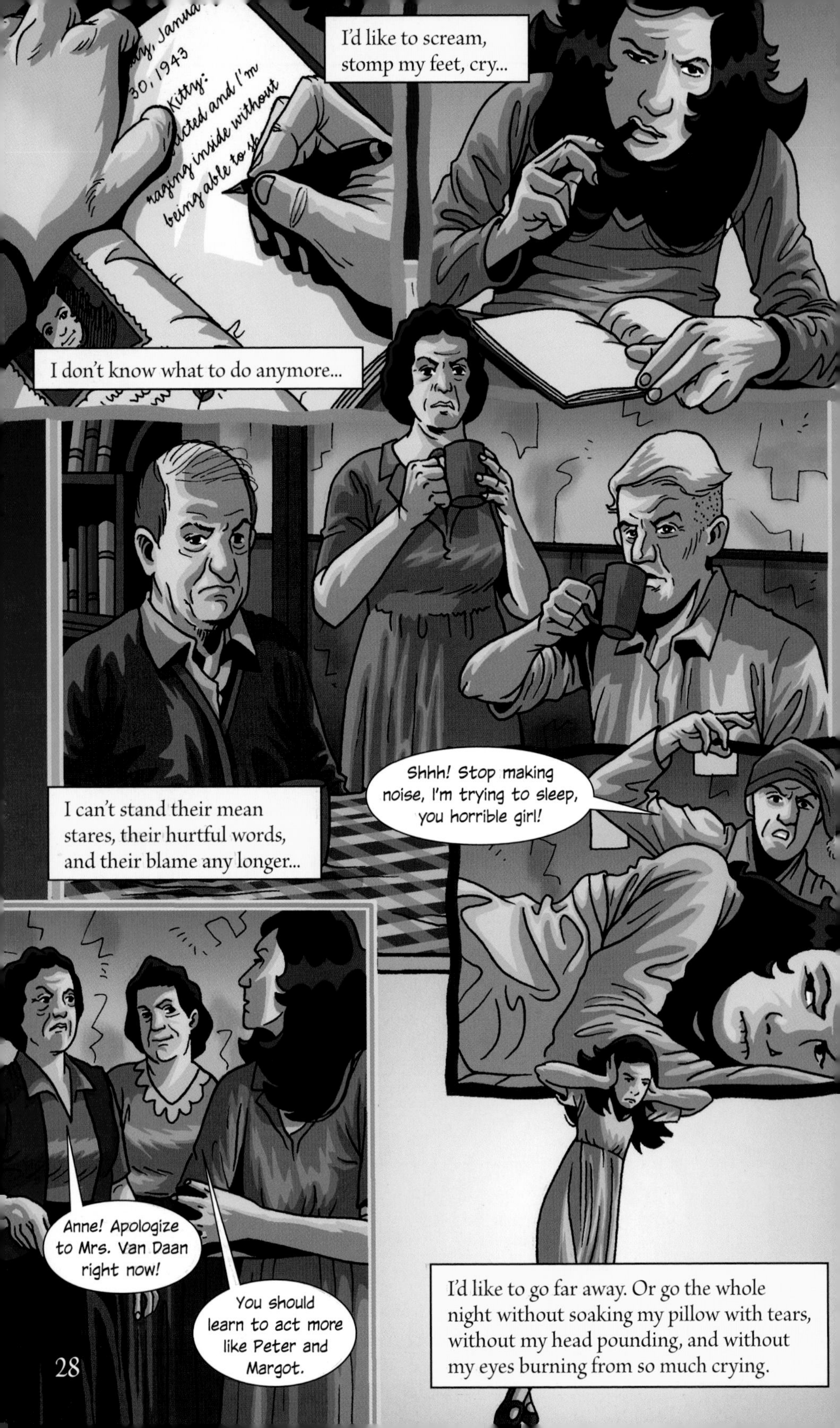

30, 1943
Kitty:
raging inside without
I'd like to scream, stomp my feet, cry...
I don't know what to do anymore...
I can't stand their mean stares, their hurtful words, and their blame any longer...
Shhh! Stop making noise, I'm trying to sleep, you horrible girl!
Anne! Apologize to Mrs. Van Daan right now!
You should learn to act more like Peter and Margot.
I'd like to go far away. Or go the whole night without soaking my pillow with tears, without my head pounding, and without my eyes burning from so much crying.

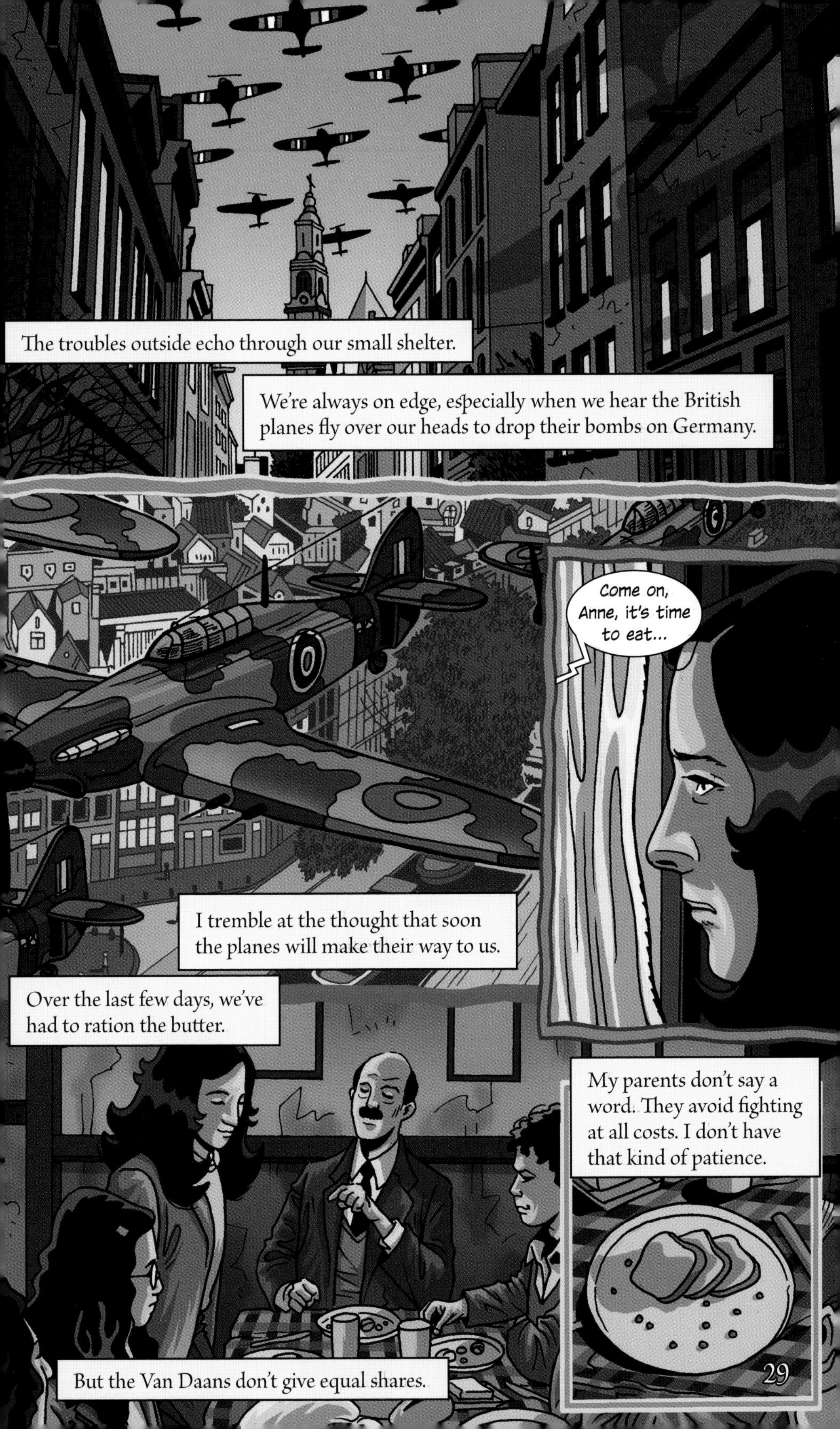

The troubles outside echo through our small shelter.
We're always on edge, especially when we hear the British planes fly over our heads to drop their bombs on Germany.
I tremble at the thought that soon the planes will make their way to us.
Come on, Anne, it's time to eat...
Over the last few days, we've had to ration the butter.
My parents don't say a word. They avoid fighting at all costs. I don't have that kind of patience.
But the Van Daans don't give equal shares.

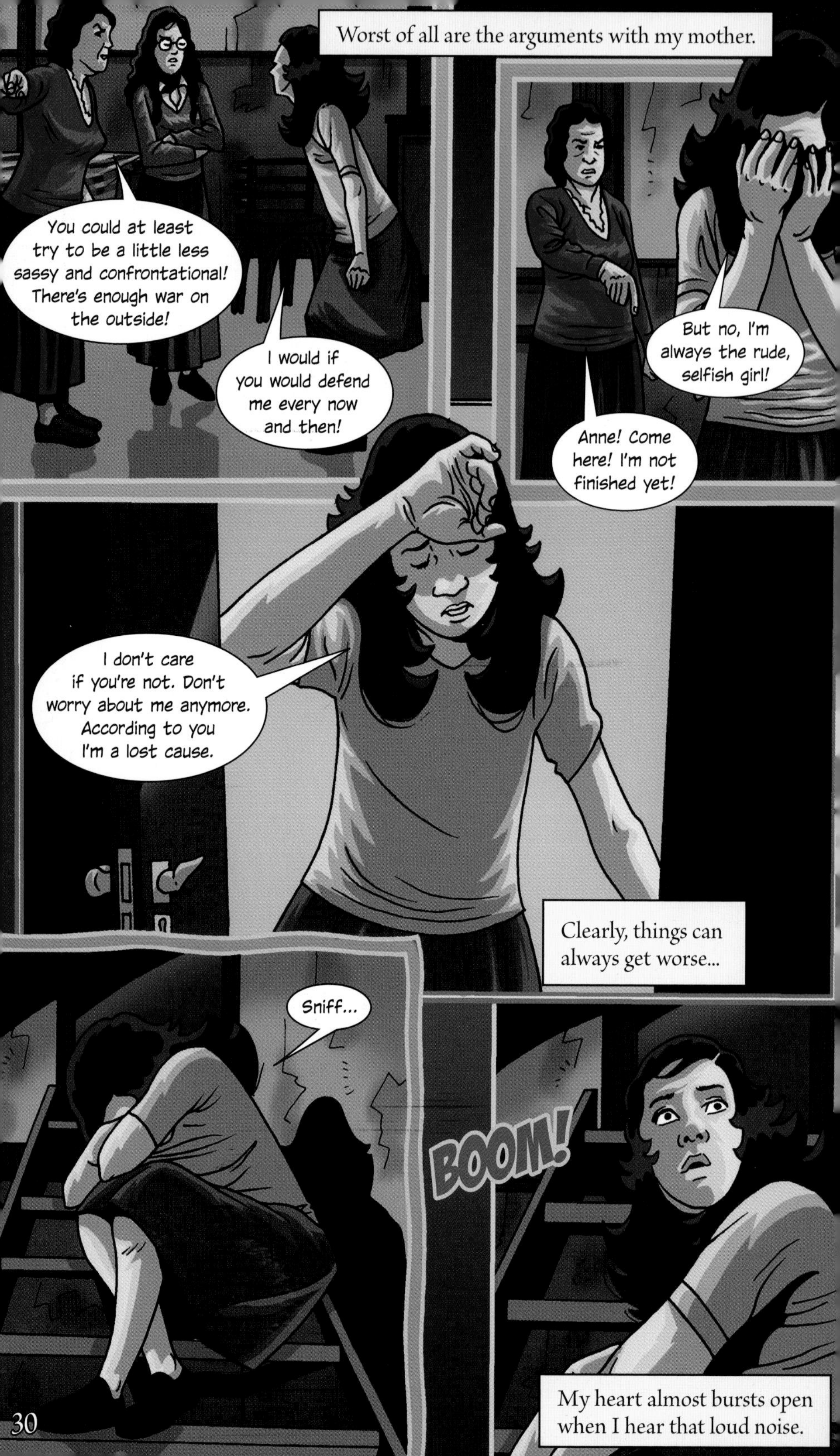
Worst of all are the arguments with my mother.
You could at least try to be a little less sassy and confrontational! There's enough war on the outside!
I would if you would defend me every now and then!
But no, I'm always the rude, selfish girl!
Anne! Come here! I'm not finished yet!
I don't care if you're not. Don't worry about me anymore. According to you I'm a lost cause.
Clearly, things can always get worse...
Sniff...
BOOM!
My heart almost bursts open when I hear that loud noise.

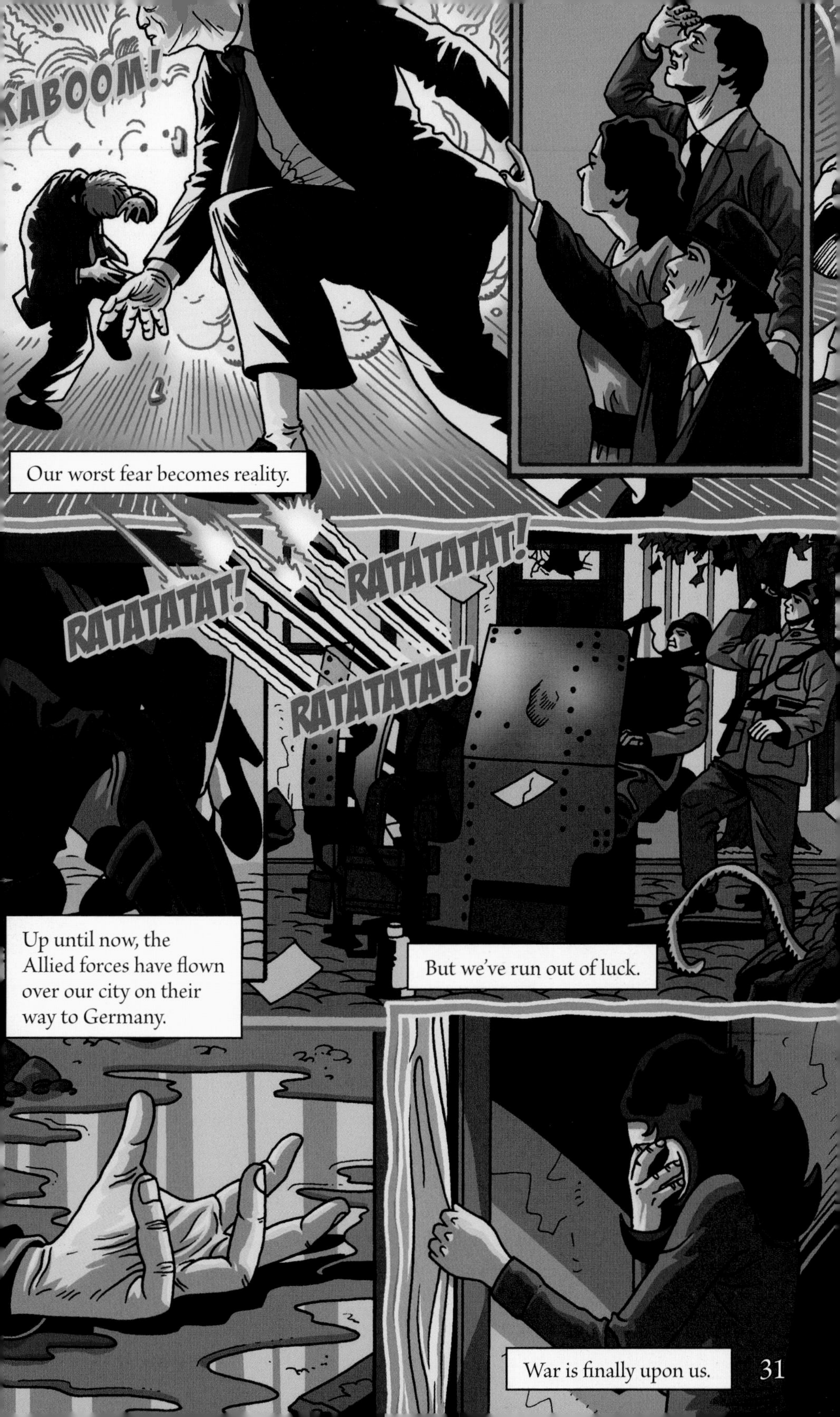
KABOOM!
Our worst fear becomes reality.
RATATATAT!
RATATATAT!
RATATATAT!
Up until now, the Allied forces have flown over our city on their way to Germany.
But we've run out of luck.
War is finally upon us.

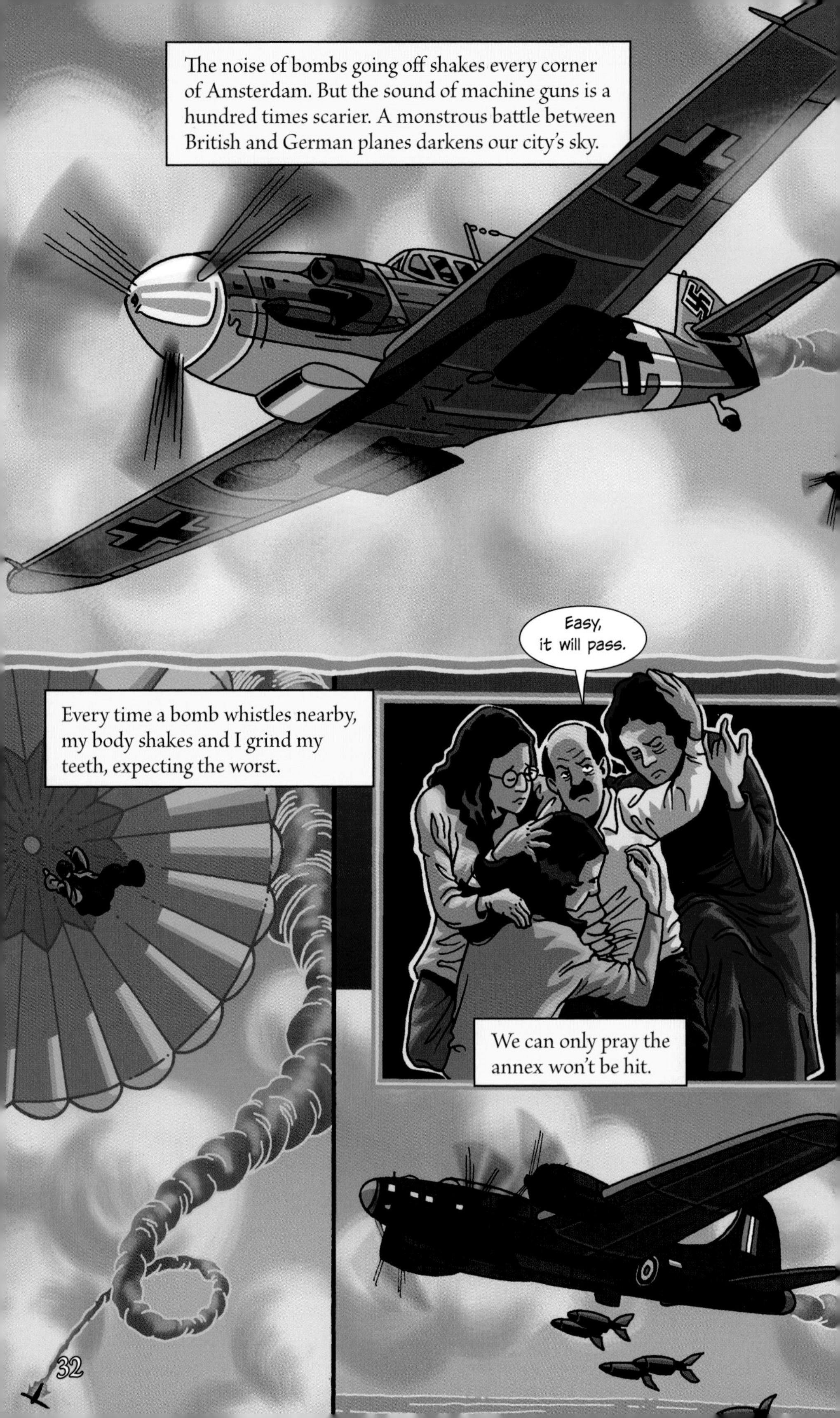
The noise of bombs going off shakes every corner of Amsterdam. But the sound of machine guns is a hundred times scarier. A monstrous battle between British and German planes darkens our city's sky.
Every time a bomb whistles nearby, my body shakes and I grind my teeth, expecting the worst.
Easy, it will pass.
We can only pray the annex won't be hit.

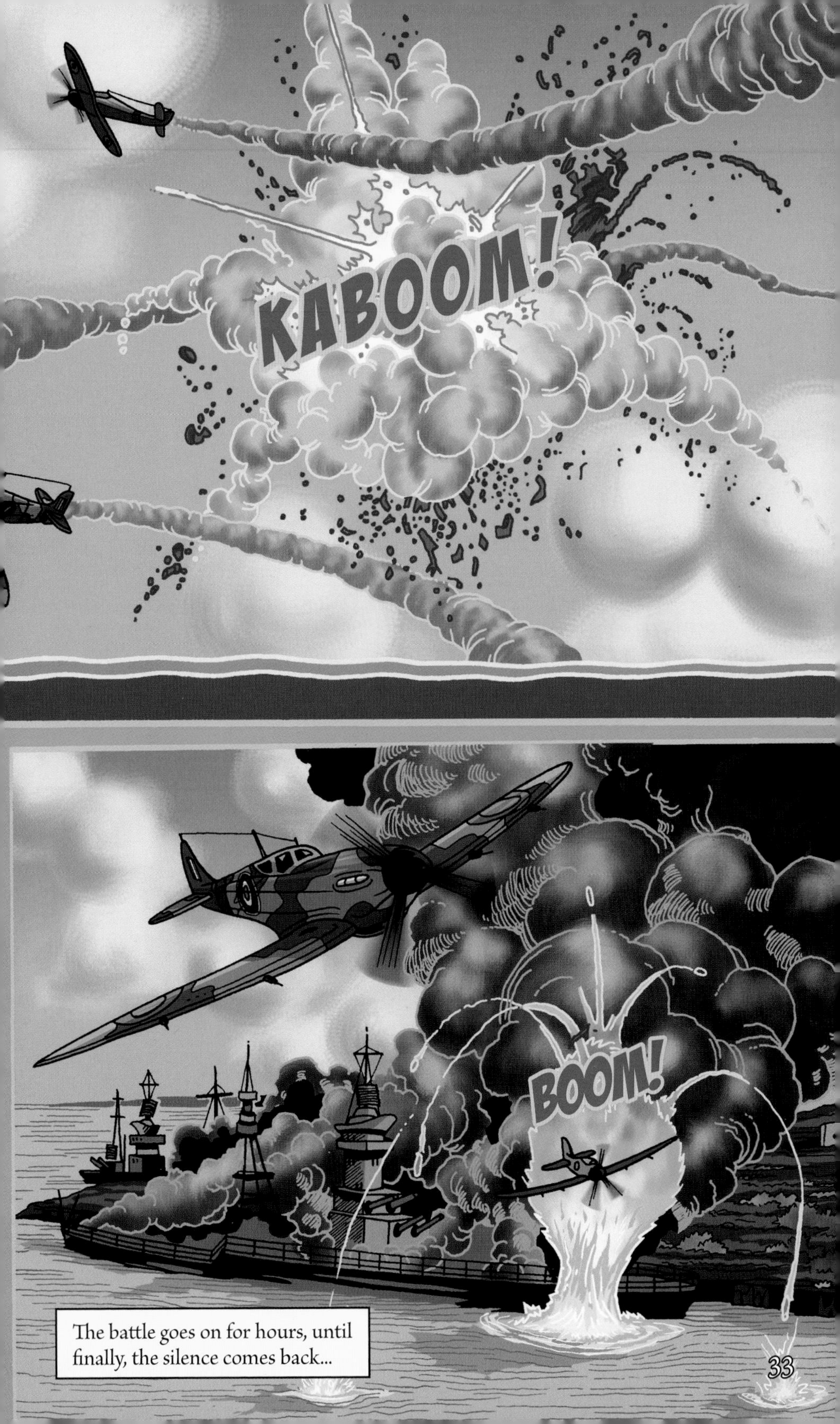
KABOOM!
BOOM!
The battle goes on for hours, until finally, the silence comes back...

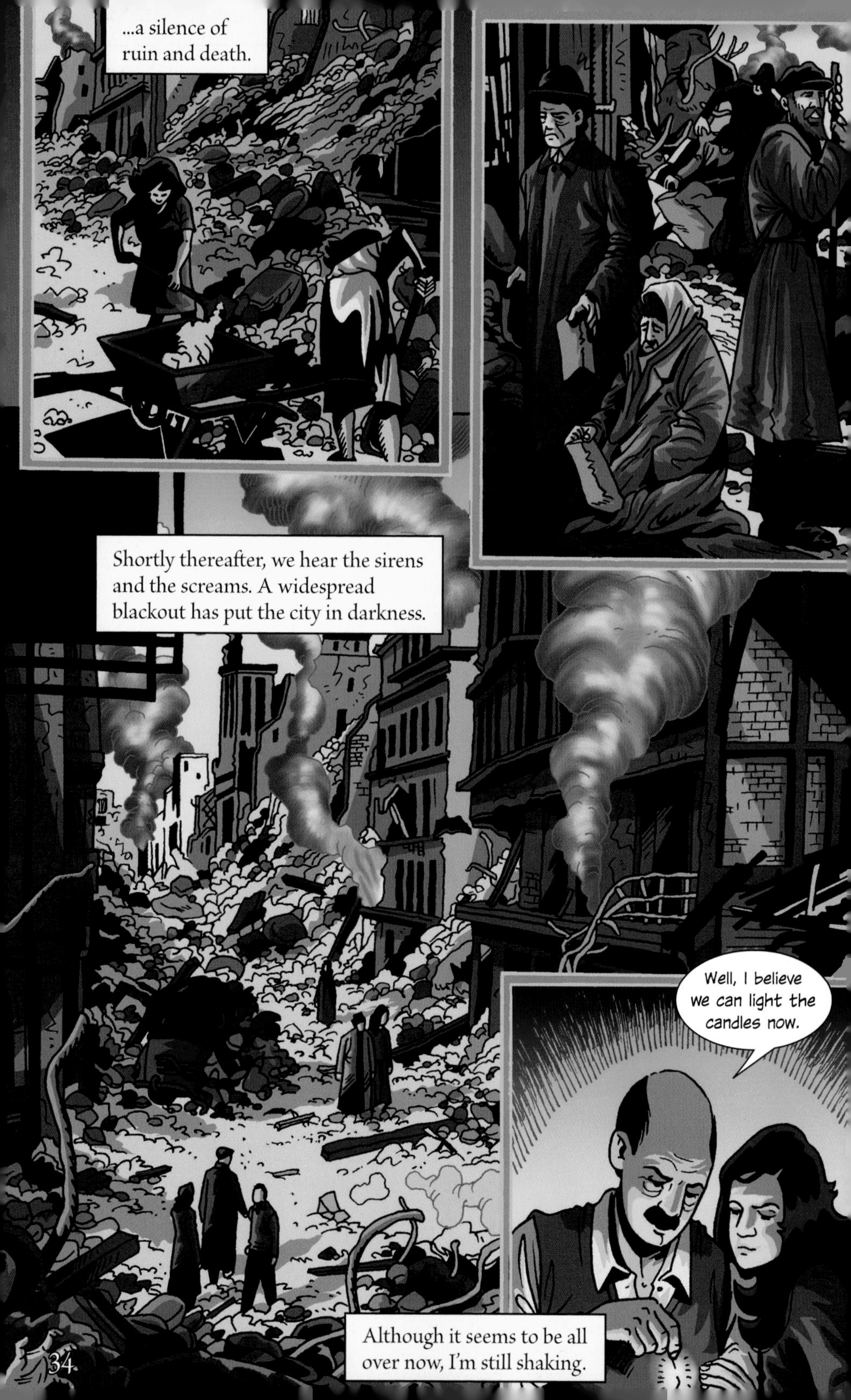
...a silence of ruin and death.
Shortly thereafter, we hear the sirens and the screams. A widespread blackout has put the city in darkness.
Well, I believe we can light the candles now.
Although it seems to be all over now, I'm still shaking.

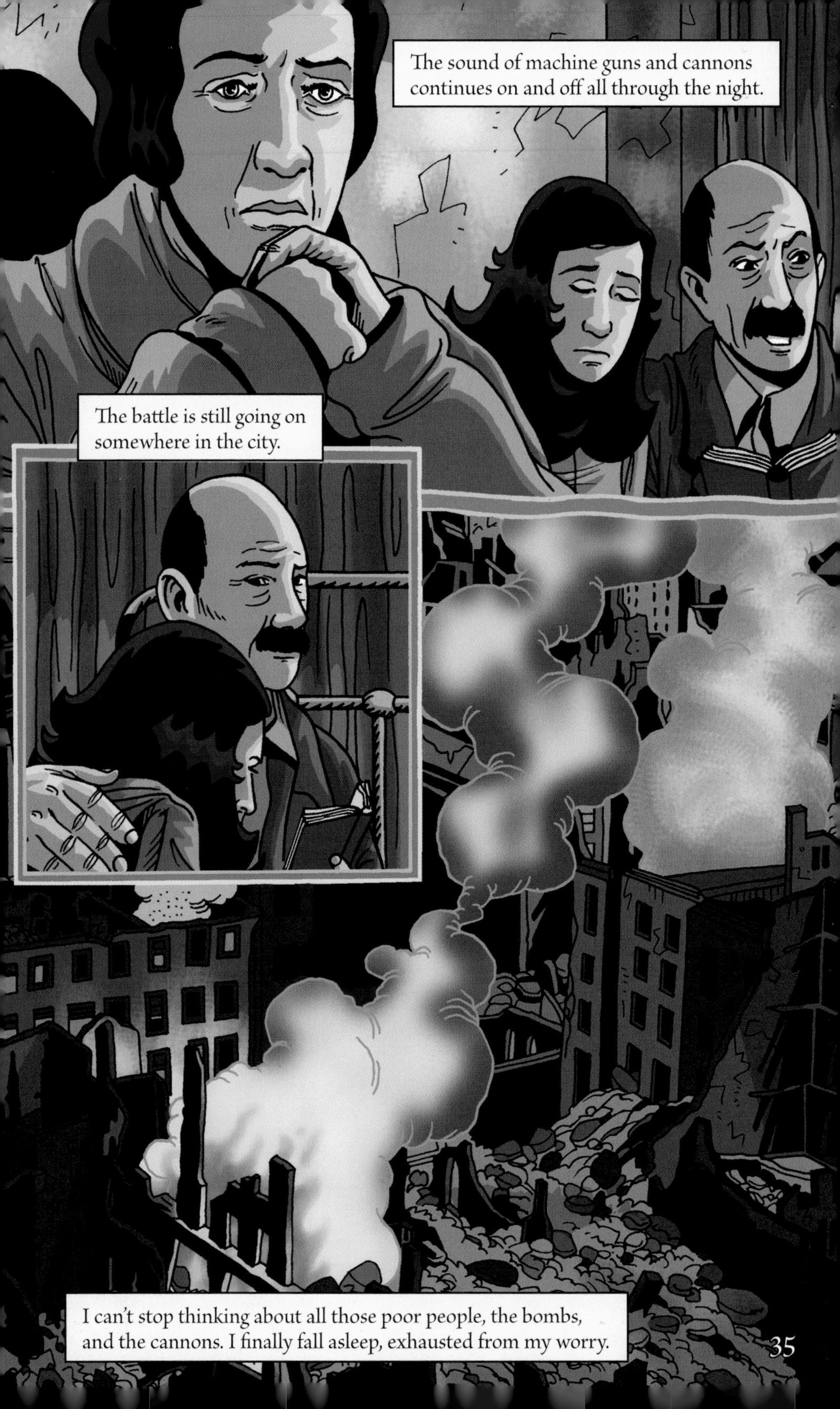
The sound of machine guns and cannons continues on and off all through the night.
The battle is still going on somewhere in the city.
I can't stop thinking about all those poor people, the bombs, and the cannons. I finally fall asleep, exhausted from my worry.

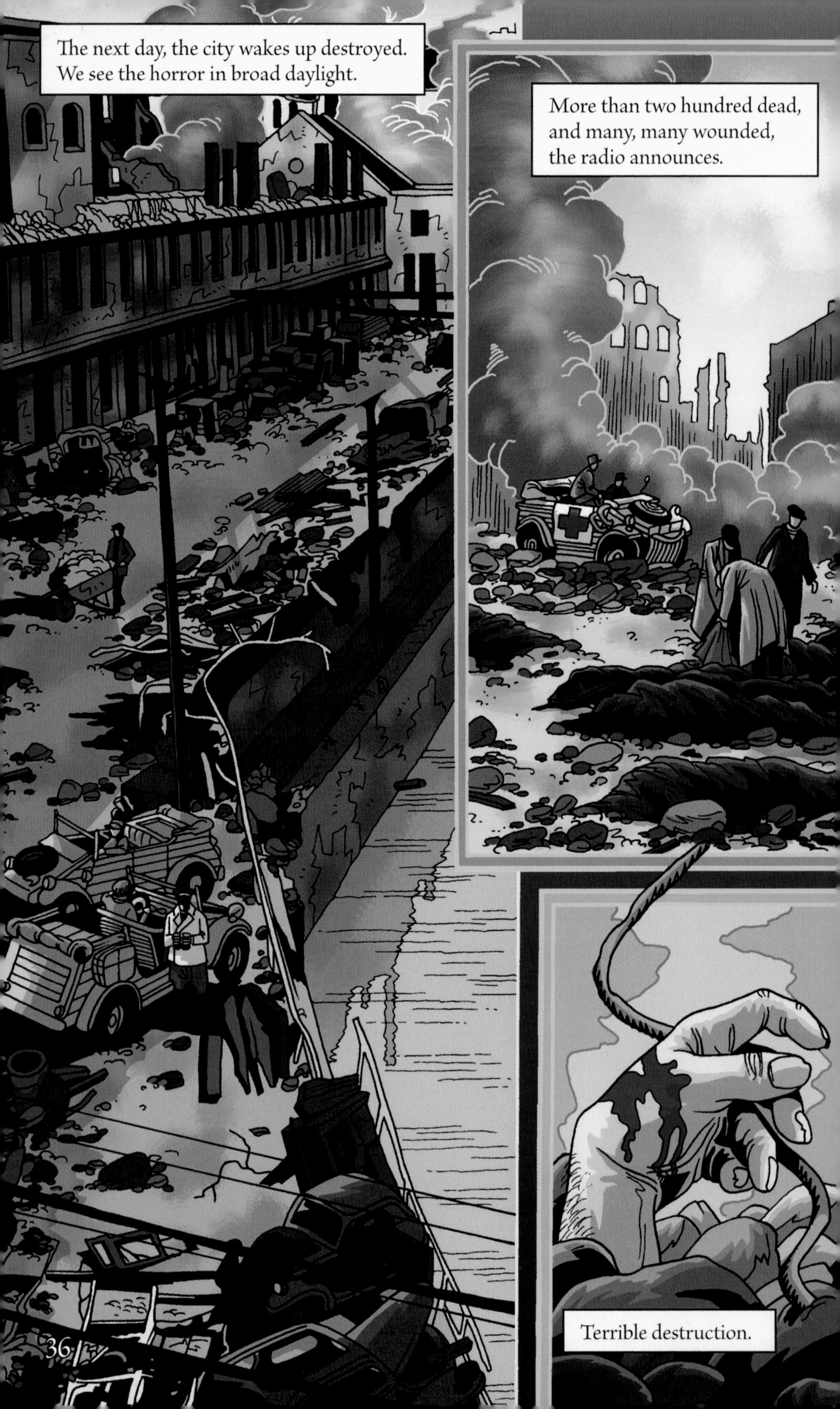
The next day, the city wakes up destroyed. We see the horror in broad daylight.
More than two hundred dead, and many, many wounded, the radio announces.
Terrible destruction.

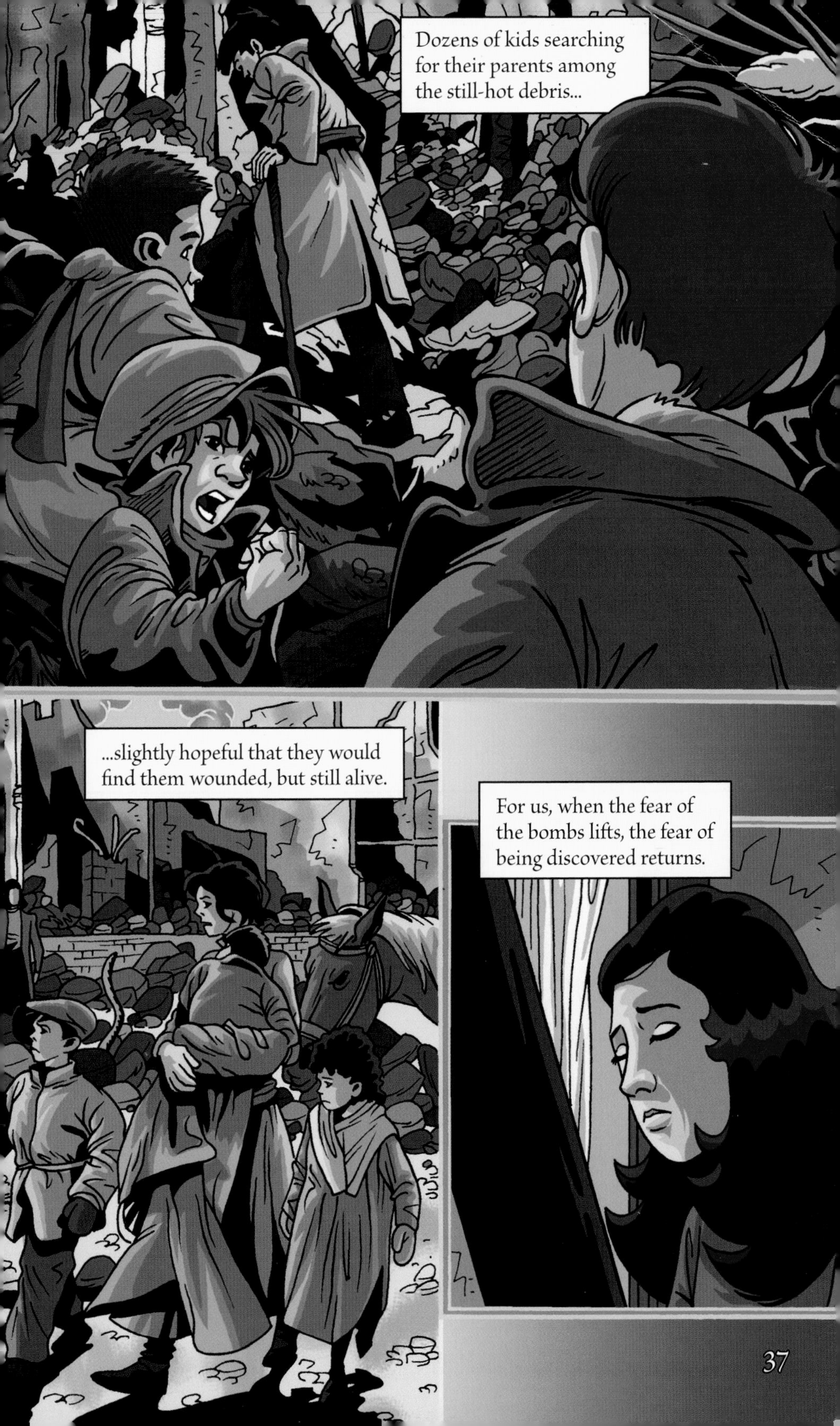
Dozens of kids searching for their parents among the still-hot debris...
...slightly hopeful that they would find them wounded, but still alive.
For us, when the fear of the bombs lifts, the fear of being discovered returns.

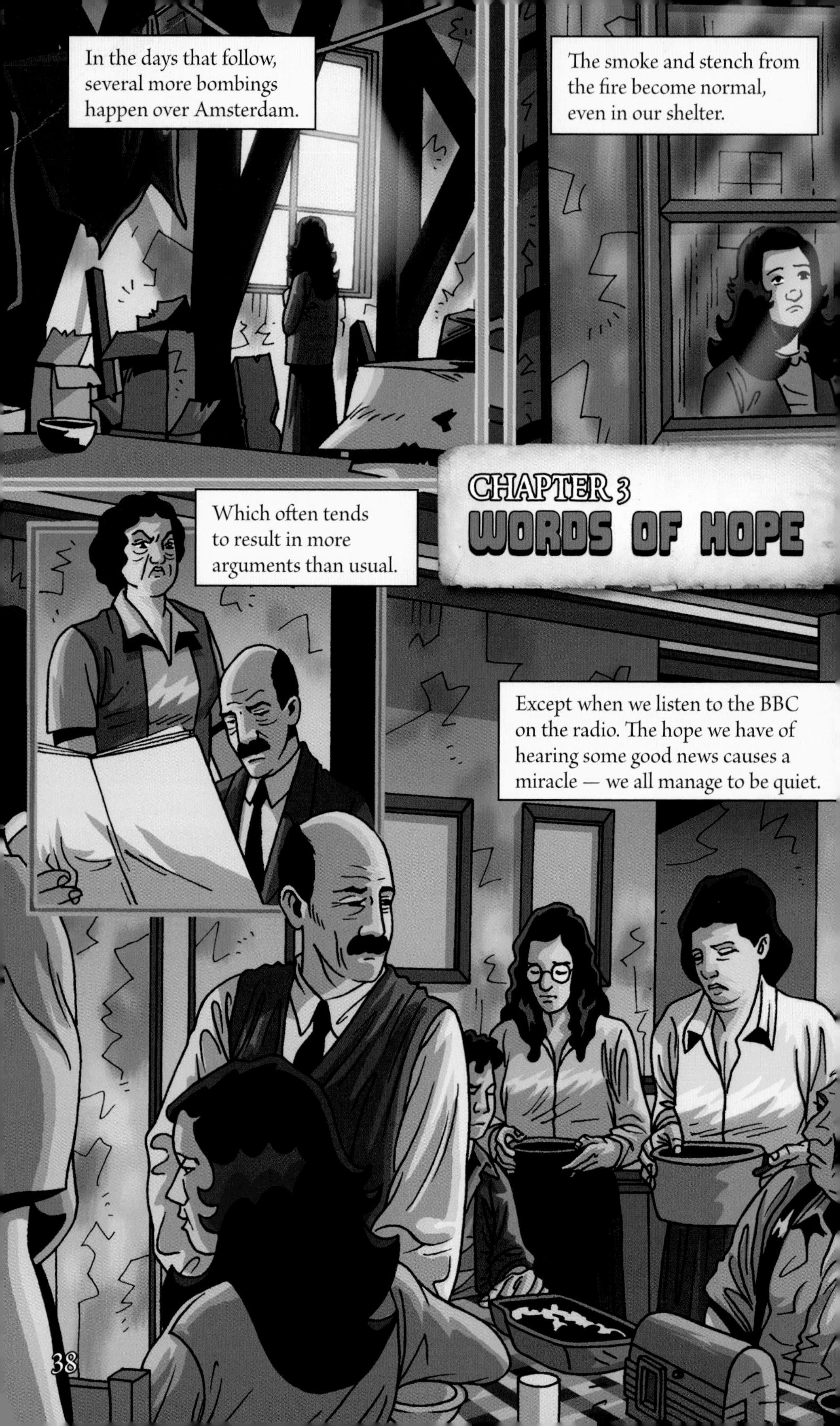

In the days that follow, several more bombings happen over Amsterdam.
The smoke and stench from the fire become normal, even in our shelter.
Which often tends to result in more arguments than usual.
CHAPTER 3
WORDS OF HOPE
Except when we listen to the BBC on the radio. The hope we have of hearing some good news causes a miracle — we all manage to be quiet.

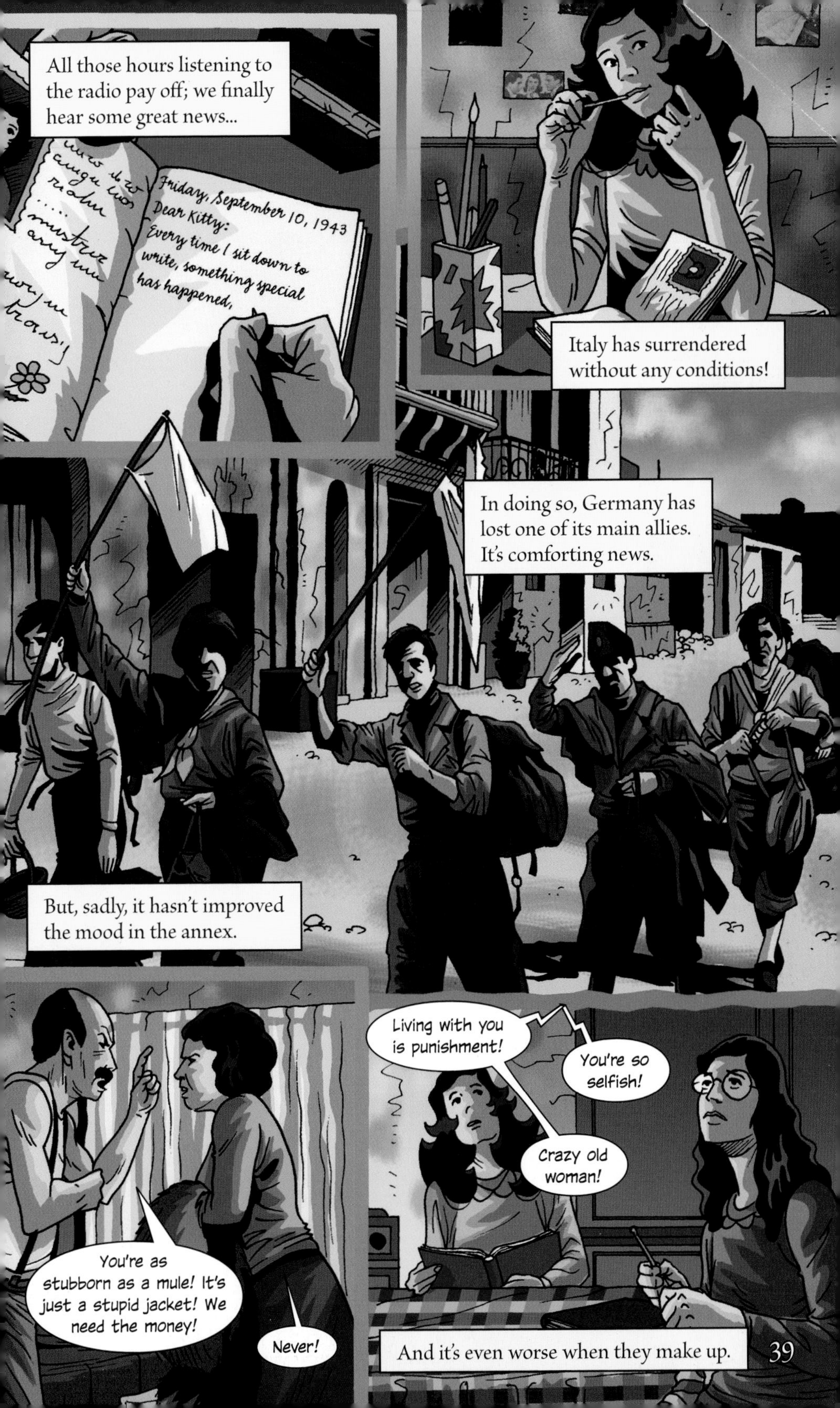
All those hours listening to the radio pay off; we finally hear some great news...
Friday, September 10, 1943
Dear Kitty:
Every time I sit down to write, something special has happened,
Italy has surrendered without any conditions!
In doing so, Germany has lost one of its main allies. It's comforting news.
But, sadly, it hasn't improved the mood in the annex.
You're as stubborn as a mule! It's just a stupid jacket! We need the money!
Never!
Living with you is punishment!
You're so selfish!
Crazy old woman!
And it's even worse when they make up.

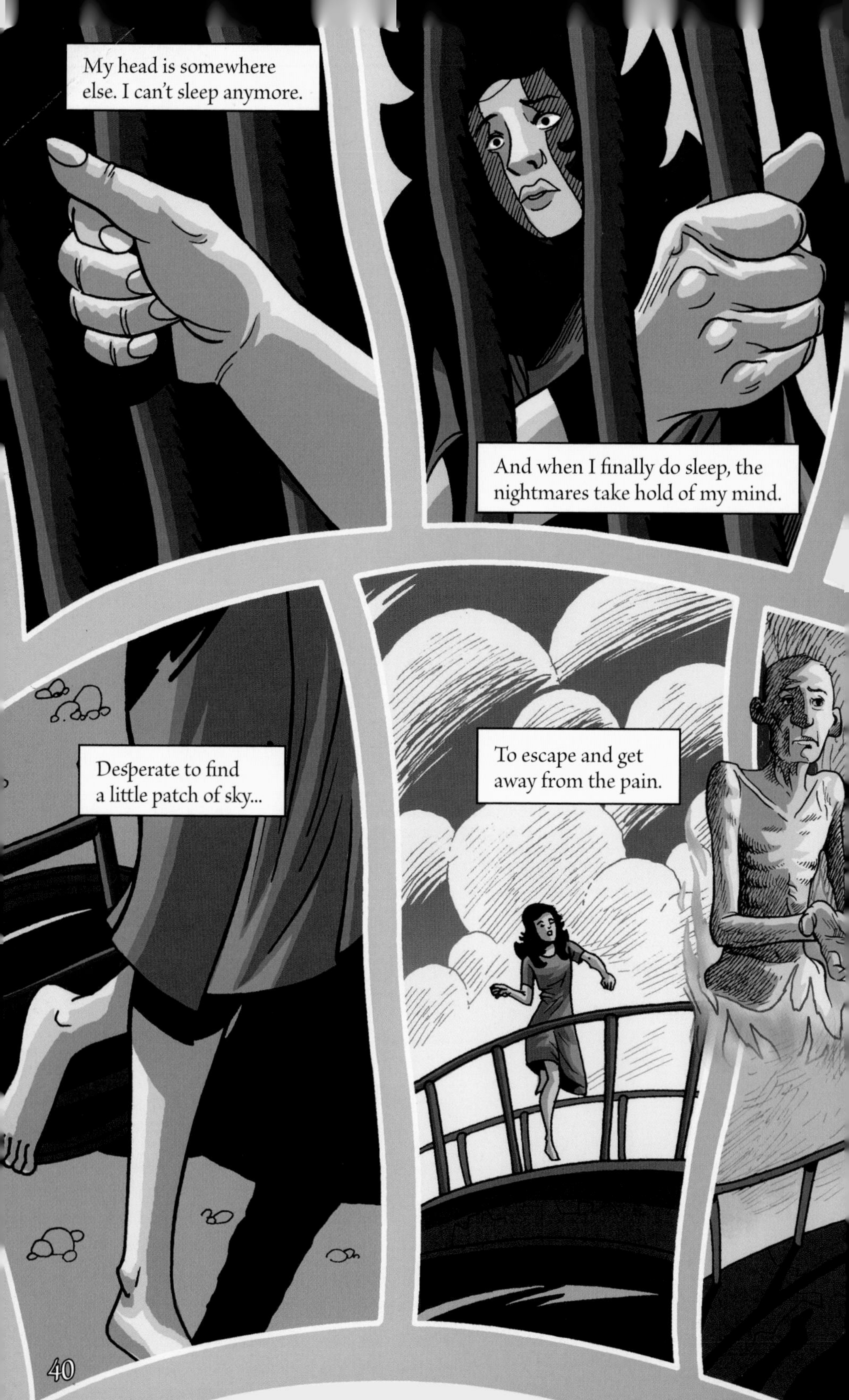

My head is somewhere else. I can't sleep anymore.
And when I finally do sleep, the nightmares take hold of my mind.
Desperate to find a little patch of sky...
To escape and get away from the pain.

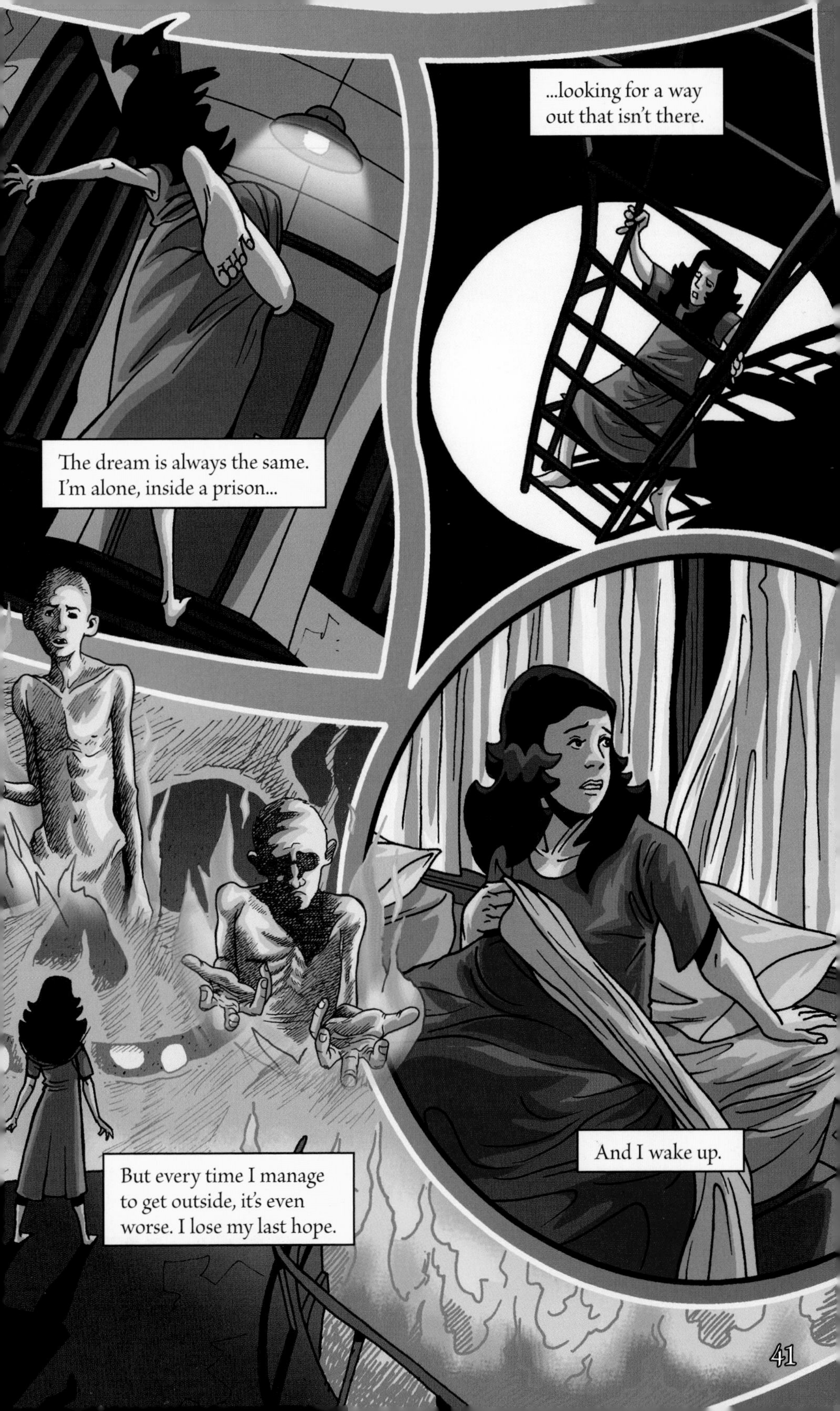

The dream is always the same. I'm alone, inside a prison...
...looking for a way out that isn't there.
But every time I manage to get outside, it's even worse. I lose my last hope.
And I wake up.

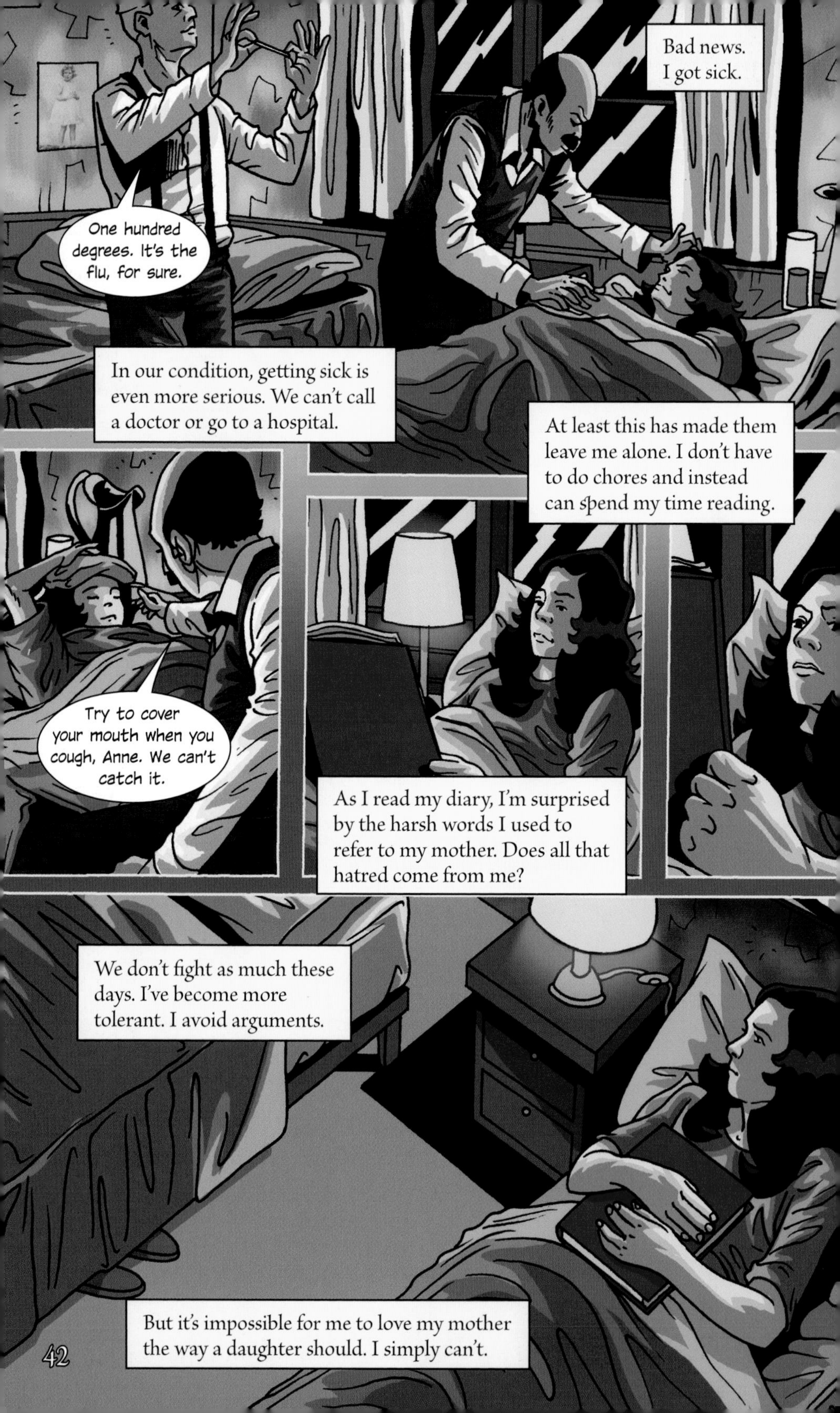

Bad news. I got sick.
One hundred degrees. It's the flu, for sure.
In our condition, getting sick is even more serious. We can't call a doctor or go to a hospital.
At least this has made them leave me alone. I don't have to do chores and instead can spend my time reading.
Try to cover your mouth when you cough, Anne. We can't catch it.
As I read my diary, I'm surprised by the harsh words I used to refer to my mother. Does all that hatred come from me?
We don't fight as much these days. I've become more tolerant. I avoid arguments.
But it's impossible for me to love my mother the way a daughter should. I simply can't.

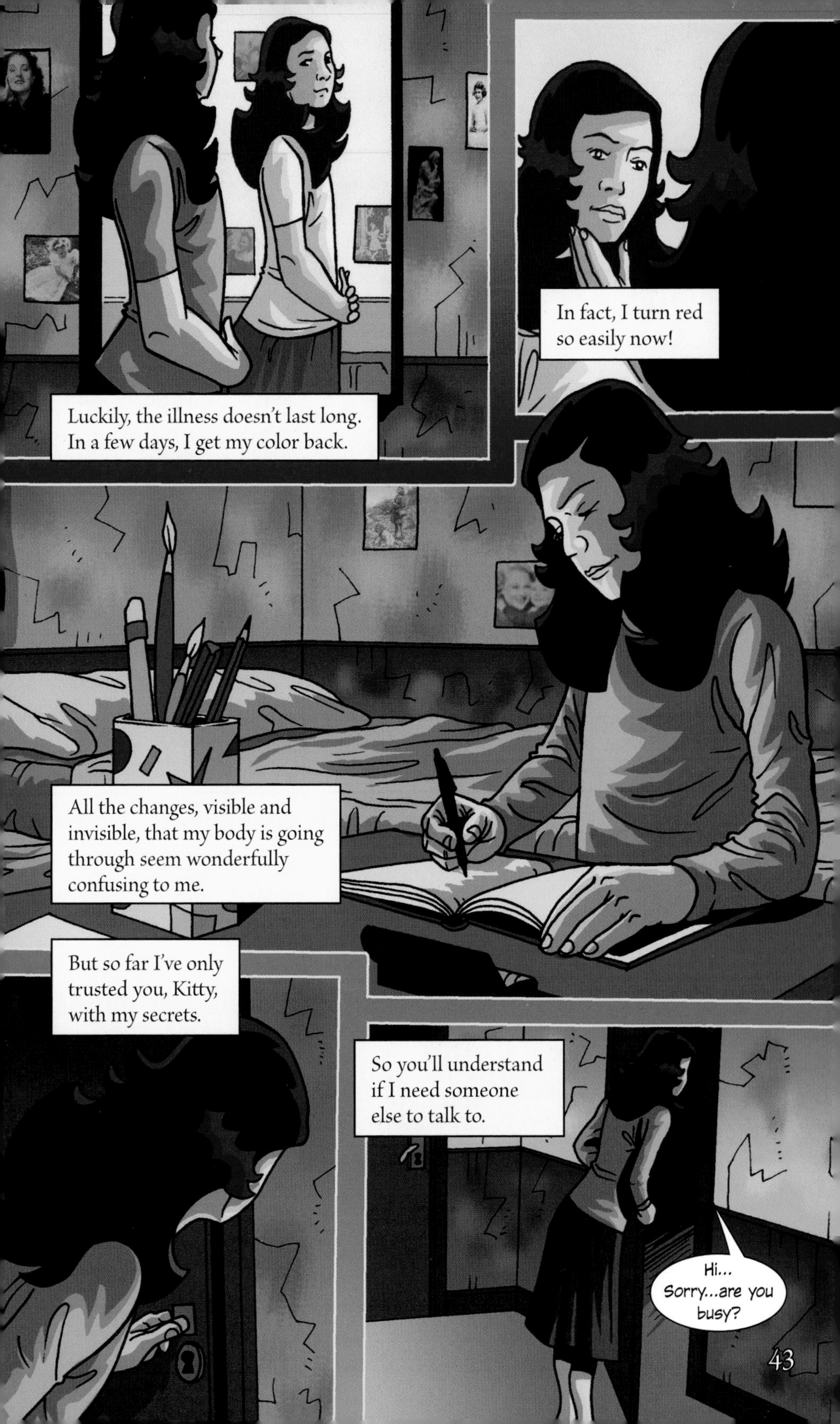
Luckily, the illness doesn't last long. In a few days, I get my color back.
In fact, I turn red so easily now!
All the changes, visible and invisible, that my body is going through seem wonderfully confusing to me.
But so far I've only trusted you, Kitty, with my secrets.
So you'll understand if I need someone else to talk to.
Hi... Sorry...are you busy?

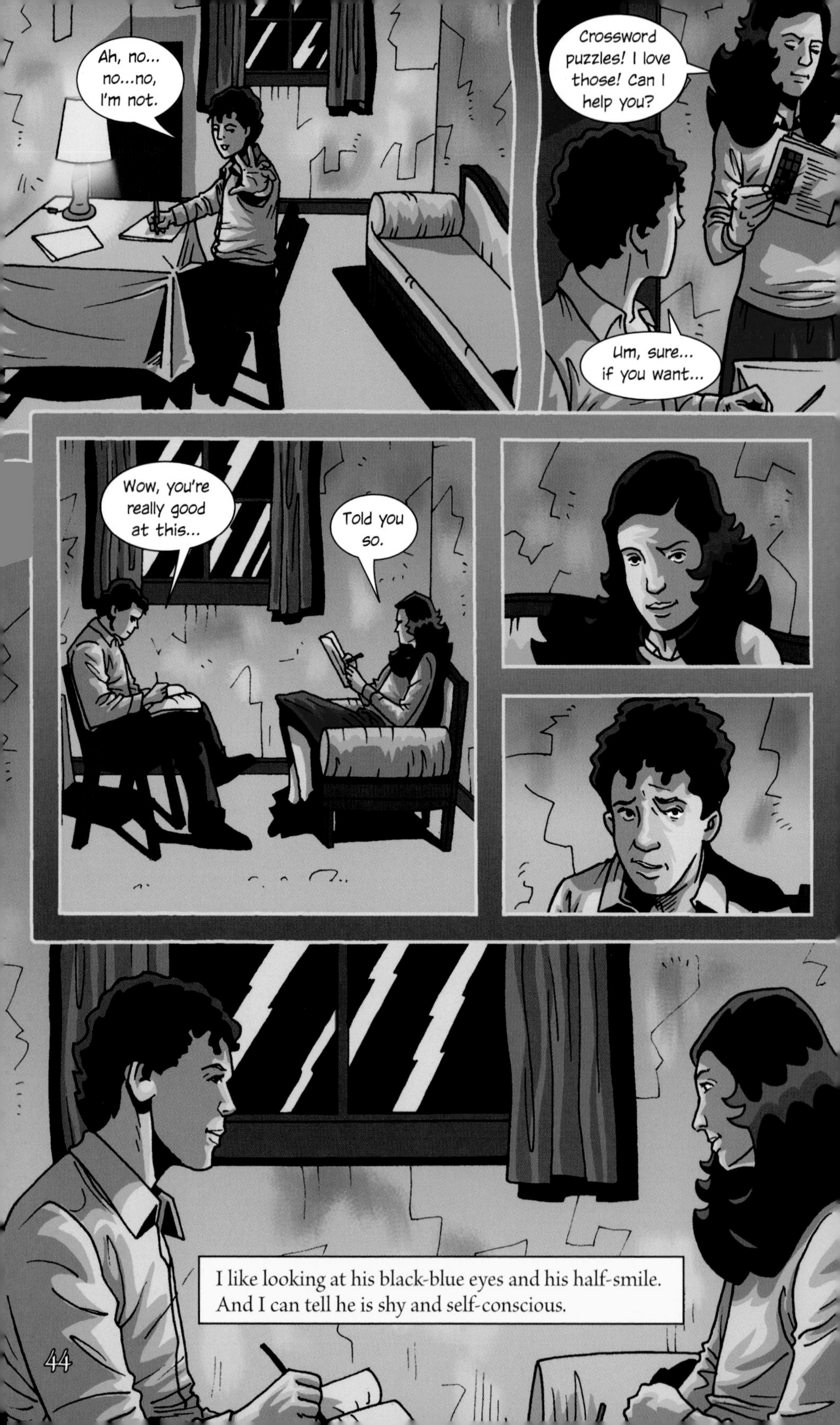

Ah, no...
no...no,
I'm not.
Crossword puzzles! I love those! Can I help you?
Um, sure... if you want...
Wow, you're really good at this...
Told you so.
I like looking at his black-blue eyes and his half-smile.
And I can tell he is shy and self-conscious.

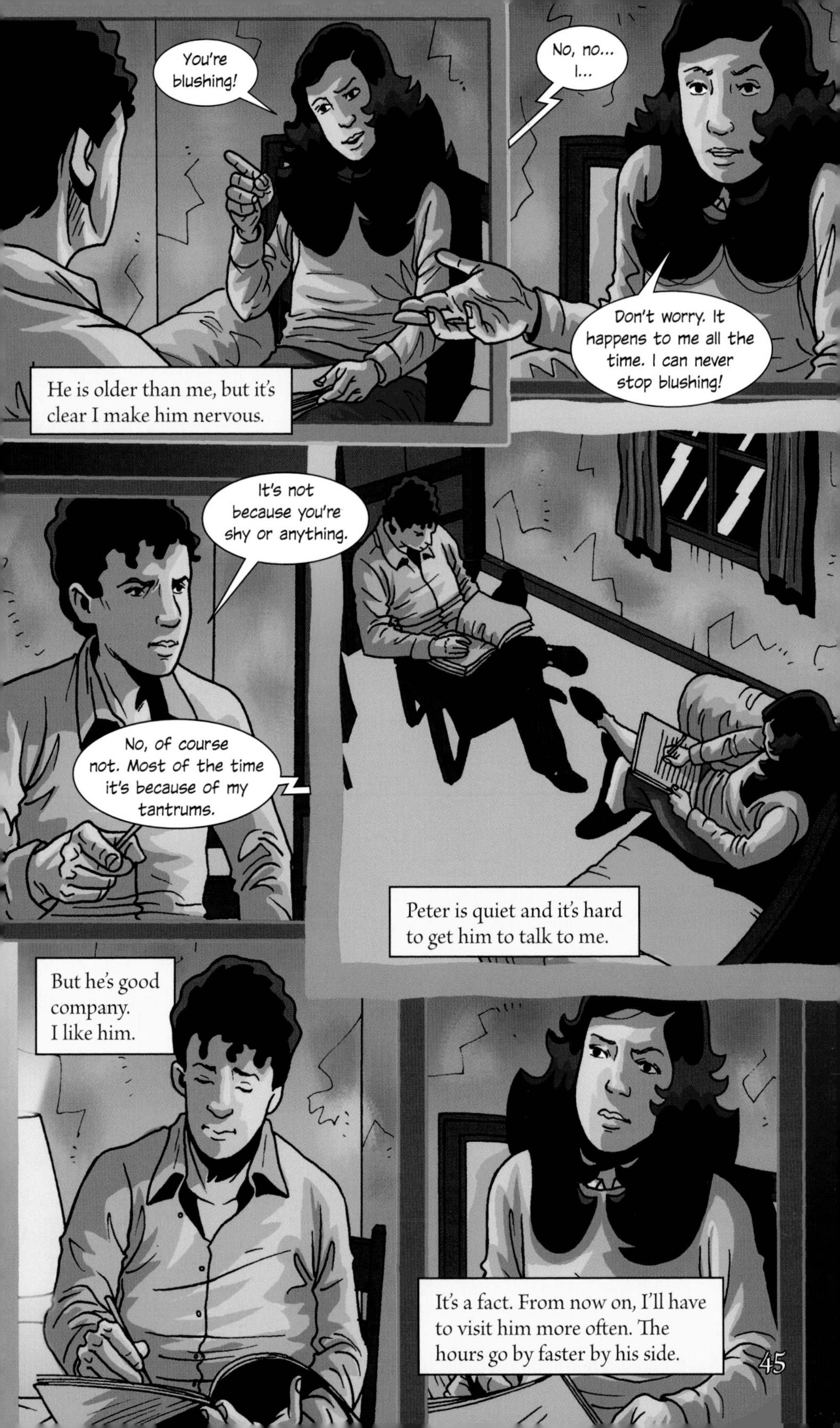

You're blushing!
He is older than me, but it's clear I make him nervous.
No, no... I...
Don't worry. It happens to me all the time. I can never stop blushing!
It's not because you're shy or anything.
No, of course not. Most of the time it's because of my tantrums.
Peter is quiet and it's hard to get him to talk to me.
But he's good company. I like him.
It's a fact. From now on, I'll have to visit him more often. The hours go by faster by his side.

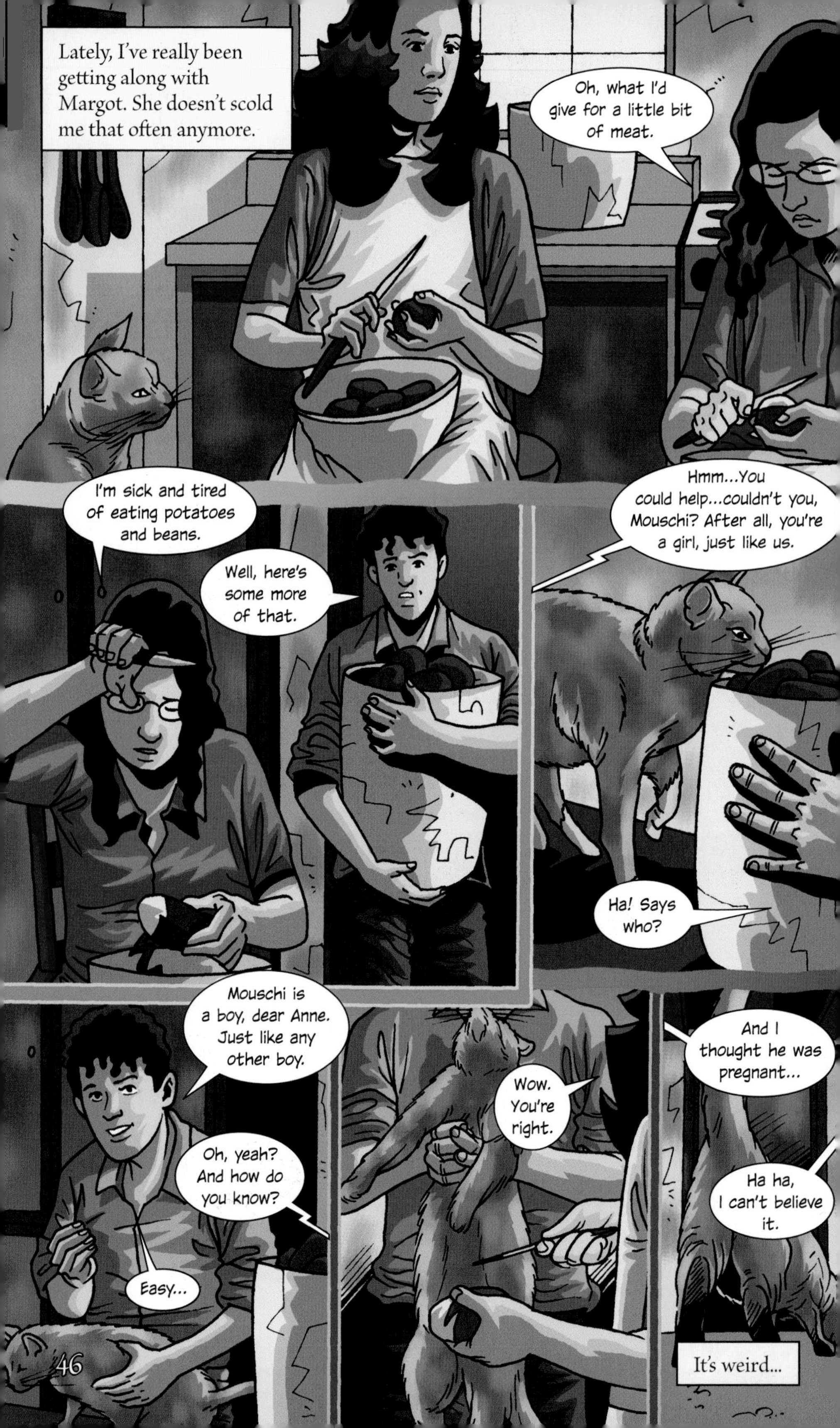

Lately, I've really been getting along with Margot. She doesn't scold me that often anymore.
Oh, what I'd give for a little bit of meat.
I'm sick and tired of eating potatoes and beans.
Well, here's some more of that.
Hmm...You could help...couldn't you, Mouschi? After all, you're a girl, just like us.
Ha! Says who?
Mouschi is a boy, dear Anne. Just like any other boy.
Oh, yeah? And how do you know?
Easy...
Wow. You're right.
And I thought he was pregnant...
Ha ha, I can't believe it.
It's weird...

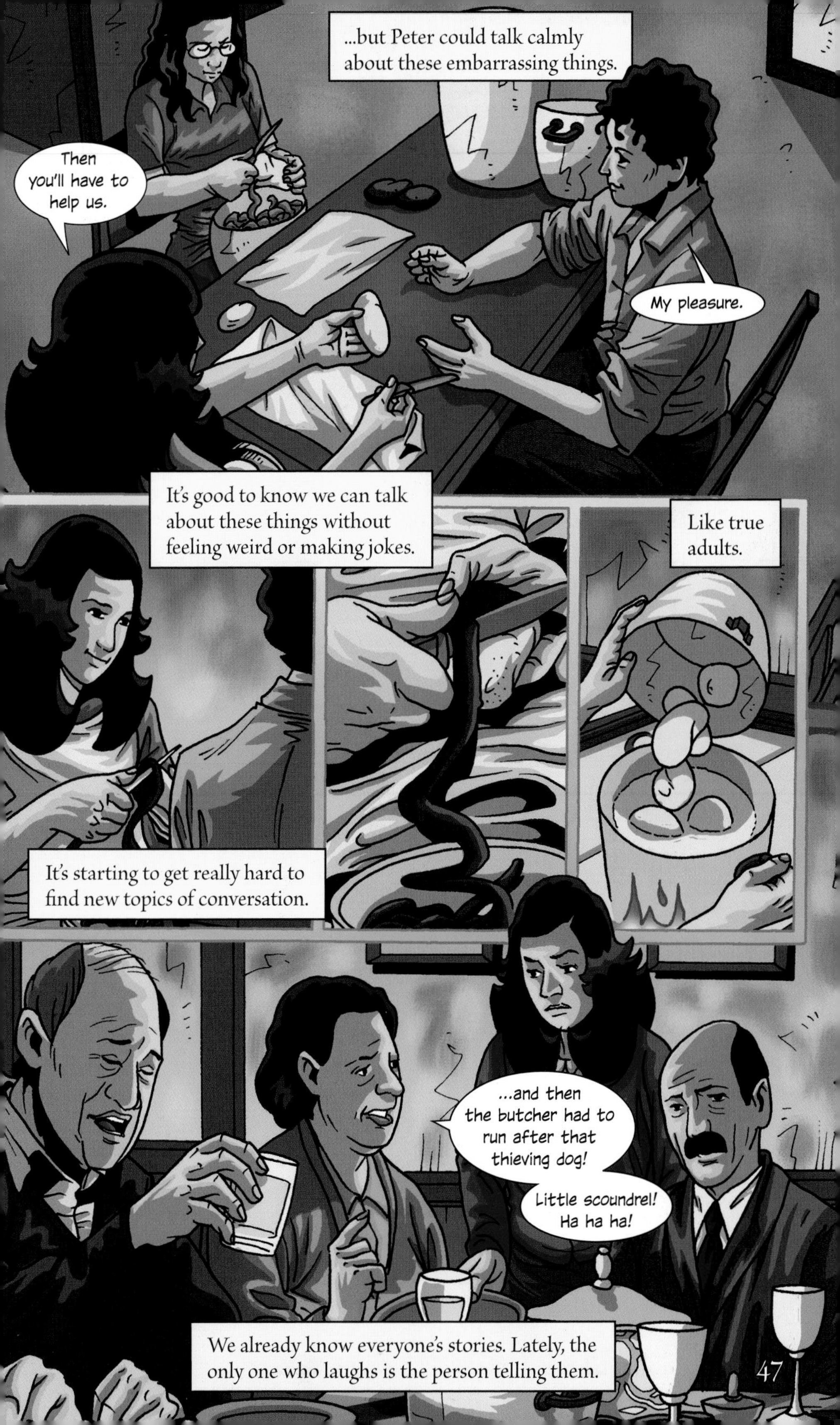
...but Peter could talk calmly about these embarrassing things.
Then you'll have to help us.
My pleasure.
It's good to know we can talk about these things without feeling weird or making jokes.
Like true adults.
It's starting to get really hard to find new topics of conversation.
...and then the butcher had to run after that thieving dog!
Little scoundrel! Ha ha ha!
We already know everyone's stories. Lately, the only one who laughs is the person telling them.

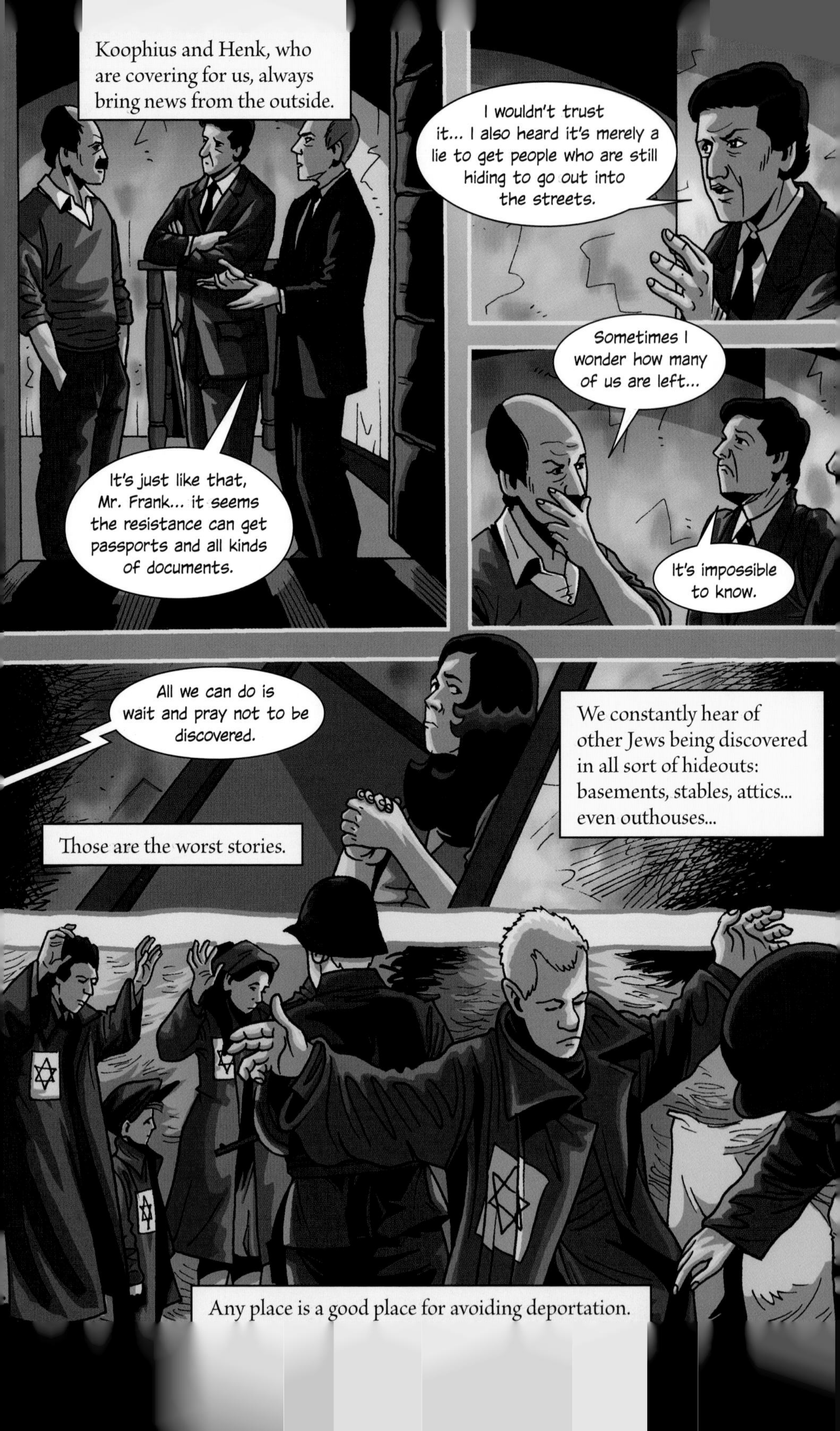
Koophius and Henk, who are covering for us, always bring news from the outside.
It's just like that, Mr. Frank... it seems the resistance can get passports and all kinds of documents.
I wouldn't trust it... I also heard it's merely a lie to get people who are still hiding to go out into the streets.
Sometimes I wonder how many of us are left...
It's impossible to know.
All we can do is wait and pray not to be discovered.
We constantly hear of other Jews being discovered in all sort of hideouts: basements, stables, attics... even outhouses...
Those are the worst stories.
Any place is a good place for avoiding deportation.

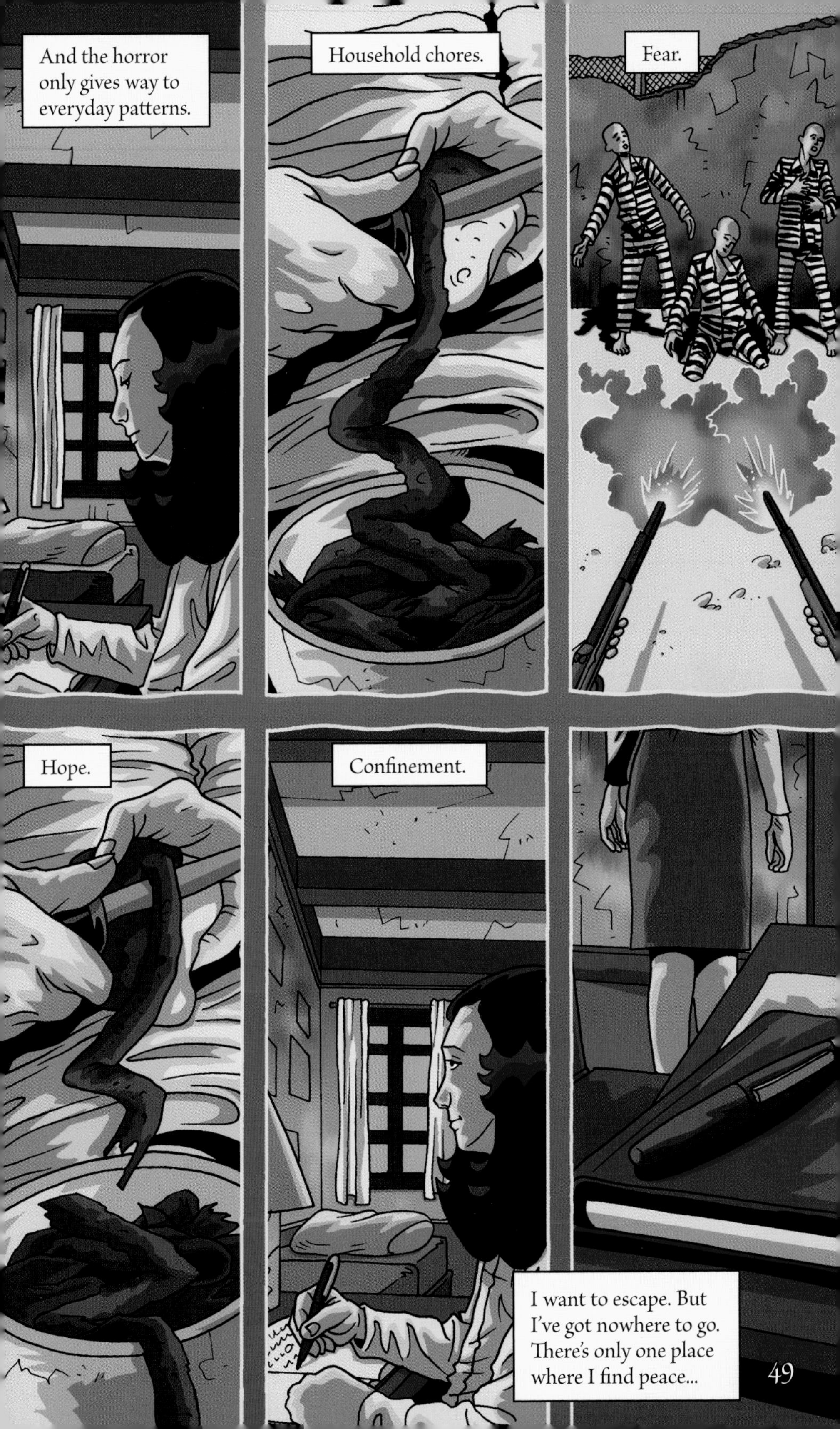
And the horror only gives way to everyday patterns.
Household chores.
Fear.
Hope.
Confinement.
I want to escape. But I've got nowhere to go. There's only one place where I find peace...

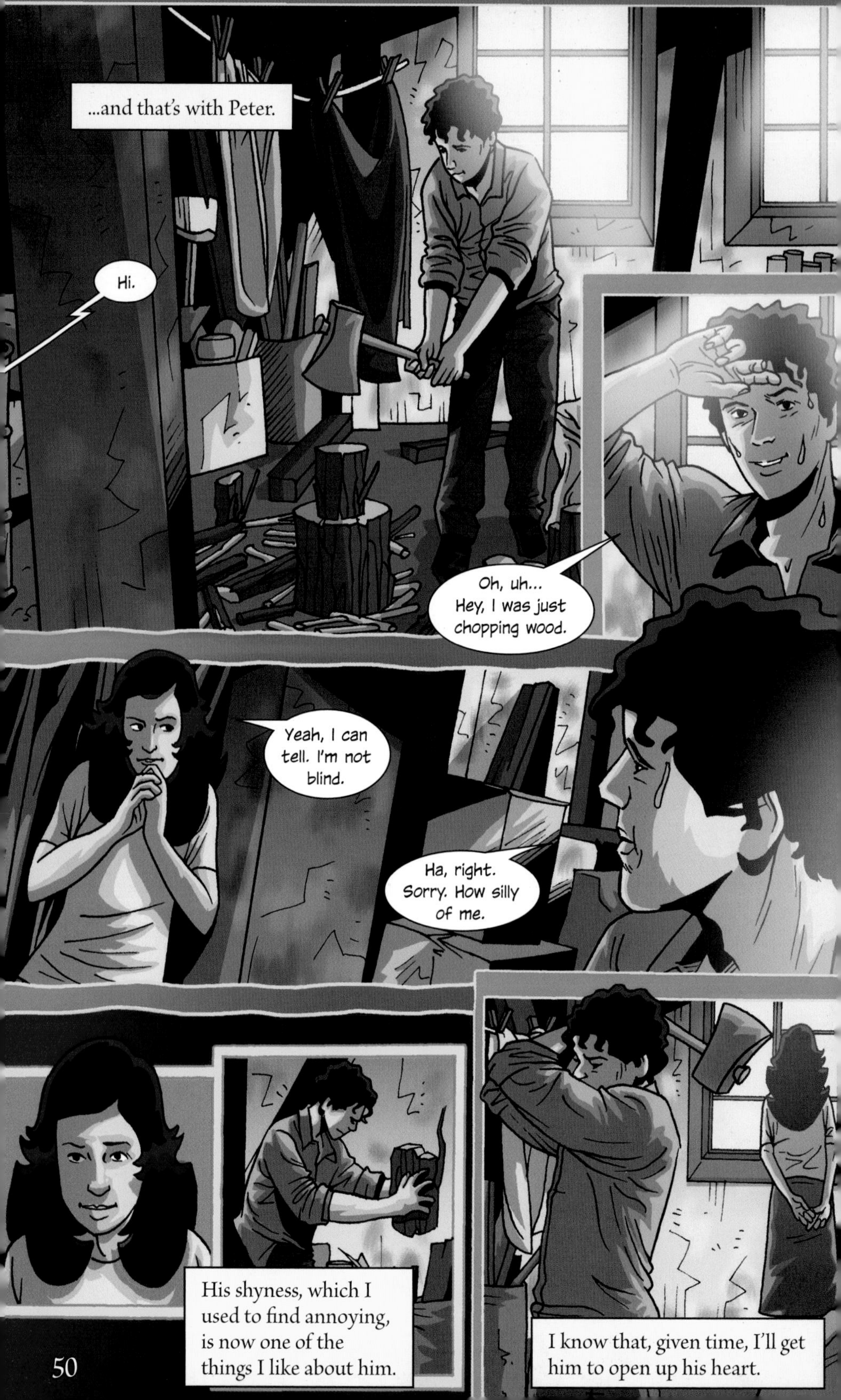
...and that's with Peter.
Hi.
Oh, uh...
Hey, I was just chopping wood.
Yeah, I can tell. I'm not blind.
Ha, right. Sorry. How silly of me.
His shyness, which I used to find annoying, is now one of the things I like about him.
I know that, given time, I'll get him to open up his heart.

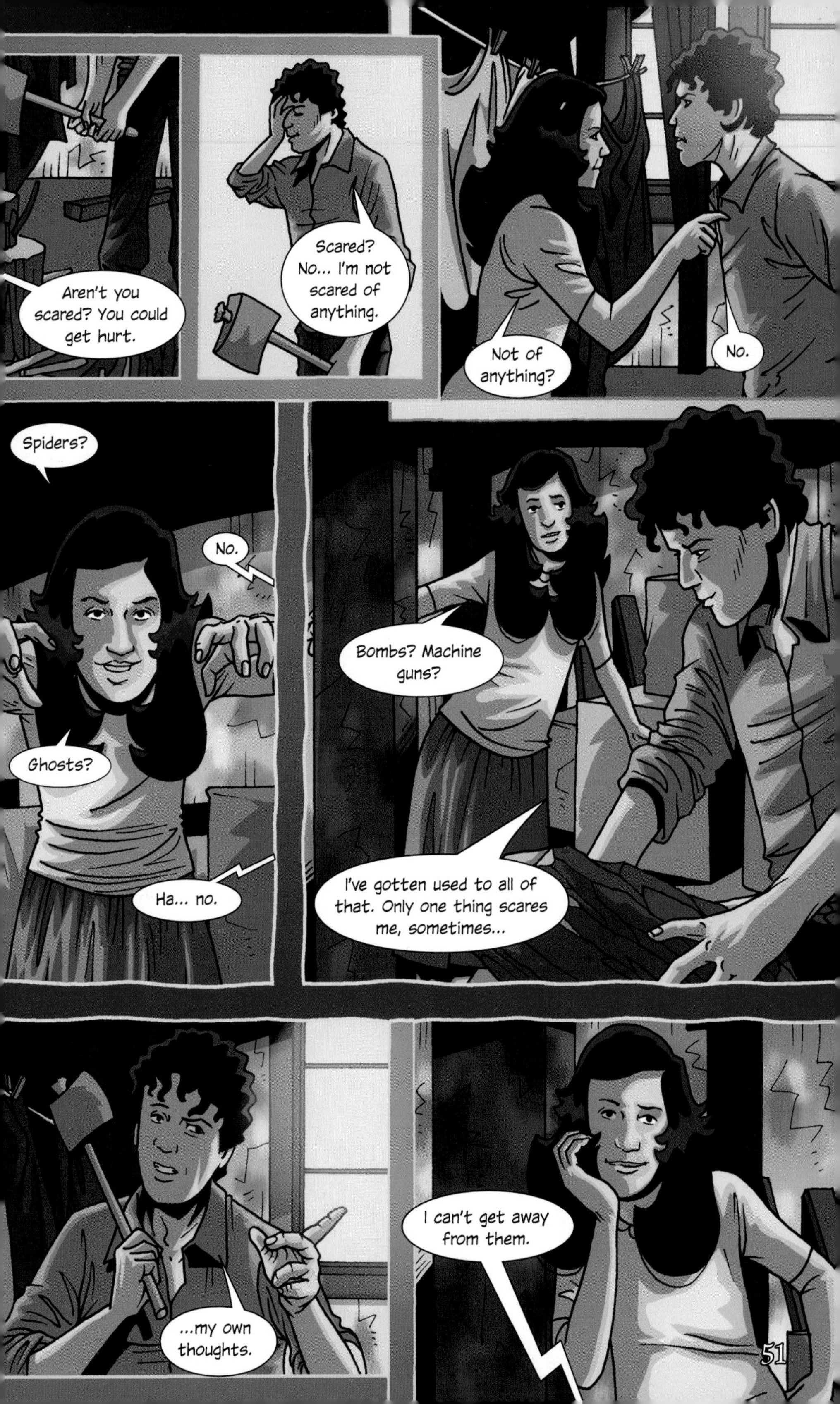
Aren't you scared? You could get hurt.
Scared? No... I'm not scared of anything.
Not of anything?
No.
Spiders?
No.
Ghosts?
Ha... no.
Bombs? Machine guns?
I've gotten used to all of that. Only one thing scares me, sometimes...
...my own thoughts.
I can't get away from them.

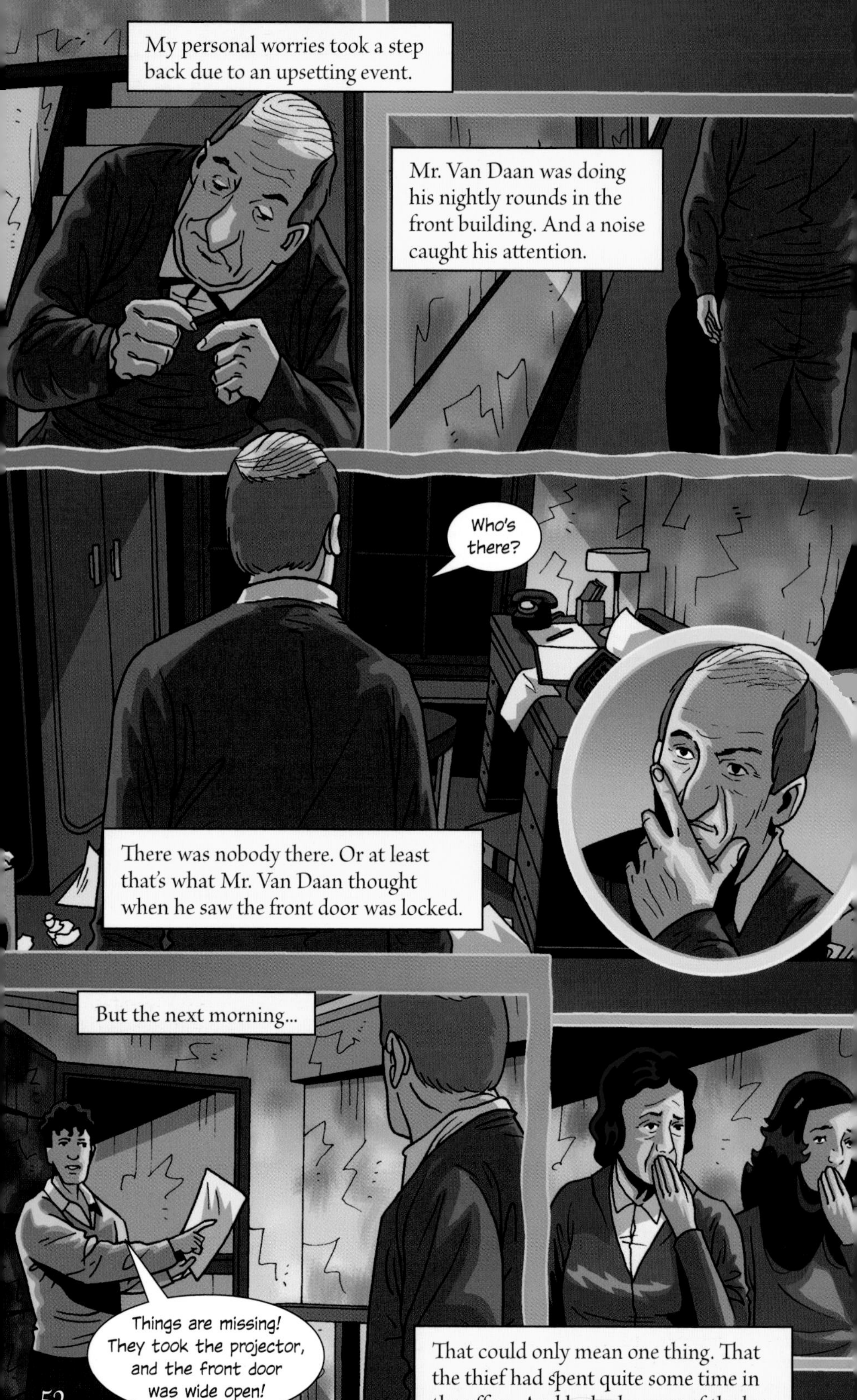
My personal worries took a step back due to an upsetting event.
Mr. Van Daan was doing his nightly rounds in the front building. And a noise caught his attention.
Who's there?
There was nobody there. Or at least that's what Mr. Van Daan thought when he saw the front door was locked.
But the next morning...
Things are missing! They took the projector, and the front door was wide open!
That could only mean one thing. That the thief had spent quite some time in the office. And he had a copy of the key.

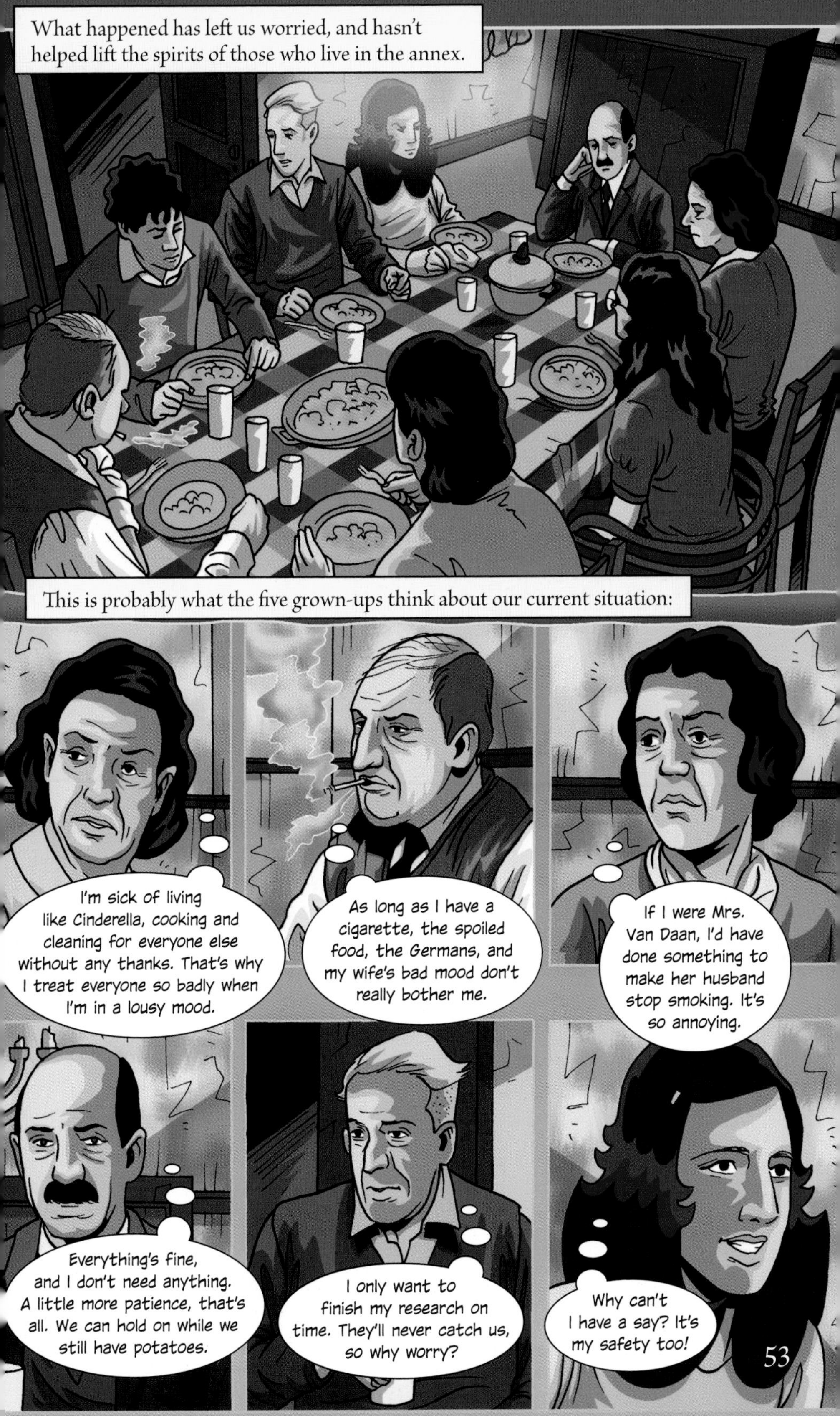
What happened has left us worried, and hasn't helped lift the spirits of those who live in the annex.
This is probably what the five grown-ups think about our current situation:
I'm sick of living like Cinderella, cooking and cleaning for everyone else without any thanks. That's why I treat everyone so badly when I'm in a lousy mood.
As long as I have a cigarette, the spoiled food, the Germans, and my wife's bad mood don't really bother me.
If I were Mrs. Van Daan, I'd have done something to make her husband stop smoking. It's so annoying.
Everything's fine, and I don't need anything. A little more patience, that's all. We can hold on while we still have potatoes.
I only want to finish my research on time. They'll never catch us, so why worry?
Why can't I have a say? It's my safety too!

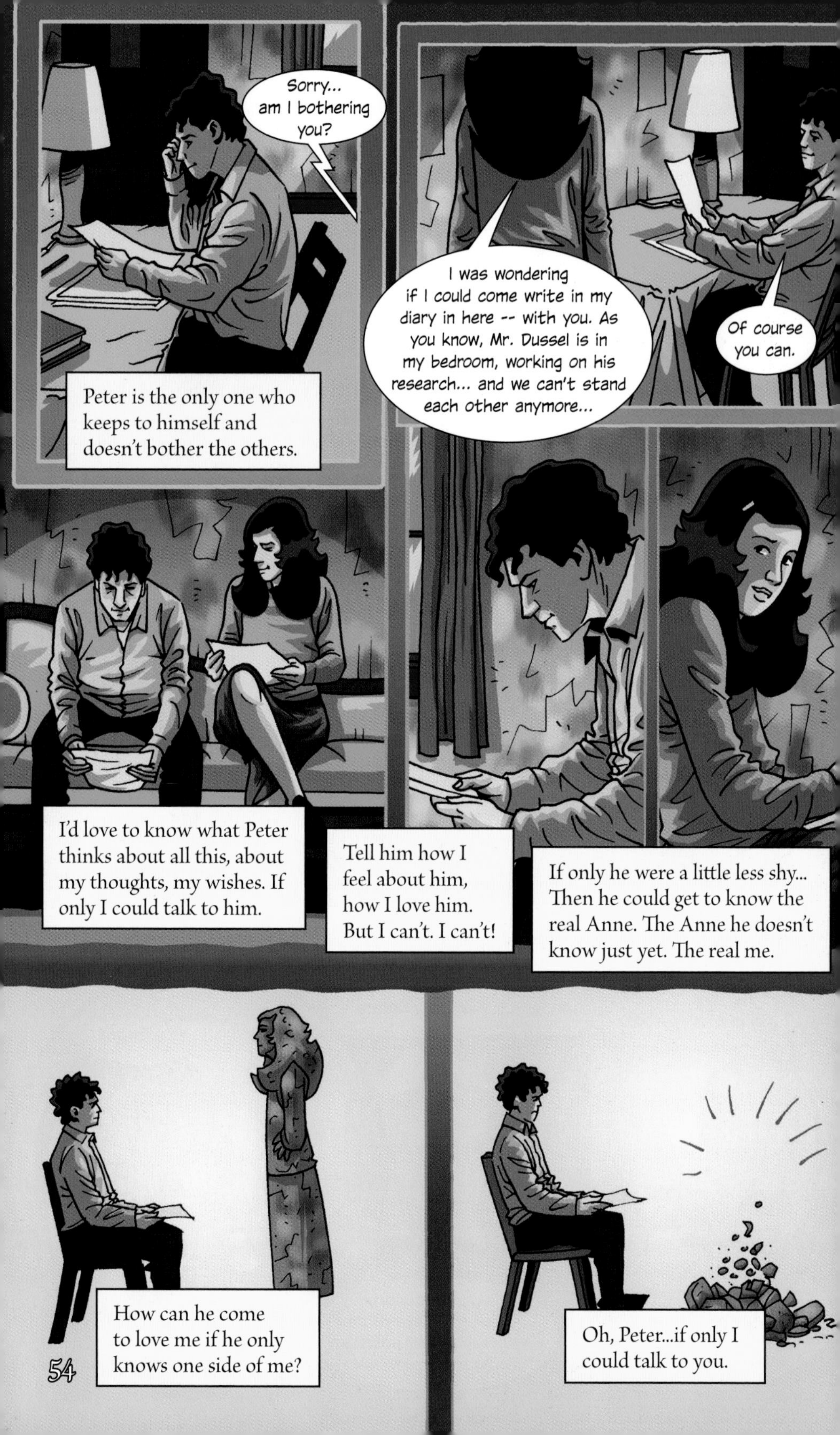
Sorry... am I bothering you?
Peter is the only one who keeps to himself and doesn't bother the others.
I was wondering if I could come write in my diary in here -- with you. As you know, Mr. Dussel is in my bedroom, working on his research... and we can't stand each other anymore...
Of course you can.
I'd love to know what Peter thinks about all this, about my thoughts, my wishes. If only I could talk to him.
Tell him how I feel about him, how I love him. But I can't. I can't!
If only he were a little less shy... Then he could get to know the real Anne. The Anne he doesn't know just yet. The real me.
How can he come to love me if he only knows one side of me?
Oh, Peter...if only I could talk to you.

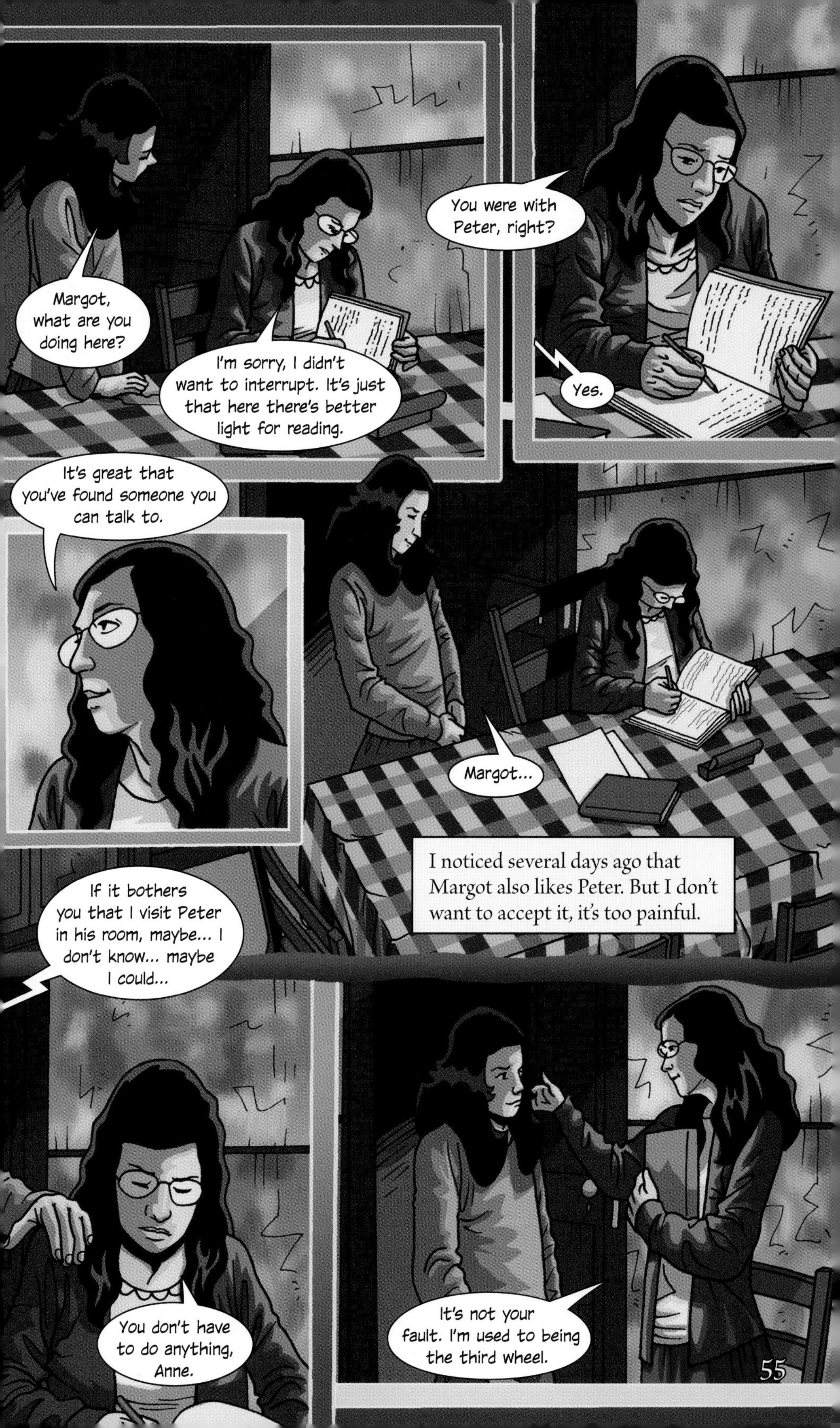
Margot, what are you doing here?
I'm sorry, I didn't want to interrupt. It's just that here there's better light for reading.
You were with Peter, right?
Yes.
It's great that you've found someone you can talk to.
Margot...
I noticed several days ago that Margot also likes Peter. But I don't want to accept it, it's too painful.
If it bothers you that I visit Peter in his room, maybe... I don't know... maybe I could...
You don't have to do anything, Anne.
It's not your fault. I'm used to being the third wheel.

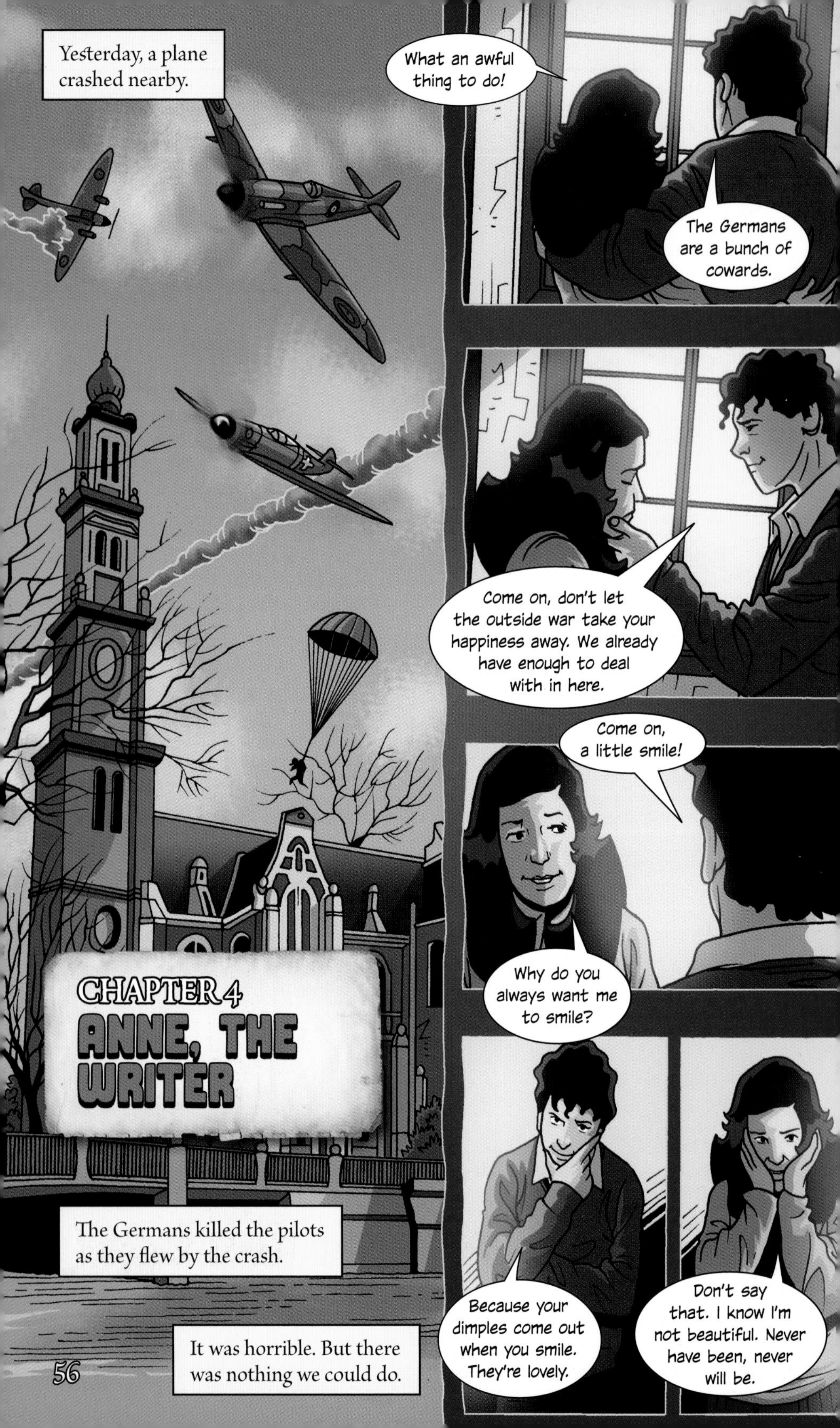

Yesterday, a plane crashed nearby.
CHAPTER 4
ANNE, THE WRITER
The Germans killed the pilots as they flew by the crash.
It was horrible. But there was nothing we could do.
What an awful thing to do!
The Germans are a bunch of cowards.
Come on, don't let the outside war take your happiness away. We already have enough to deal with in here.
Come on, a little smile!
Why do you always want me to smile?
Because your dimples come out when you smile. They're lovely.
Don't say that. I know I'm not beautiful. Never have been, never will be.

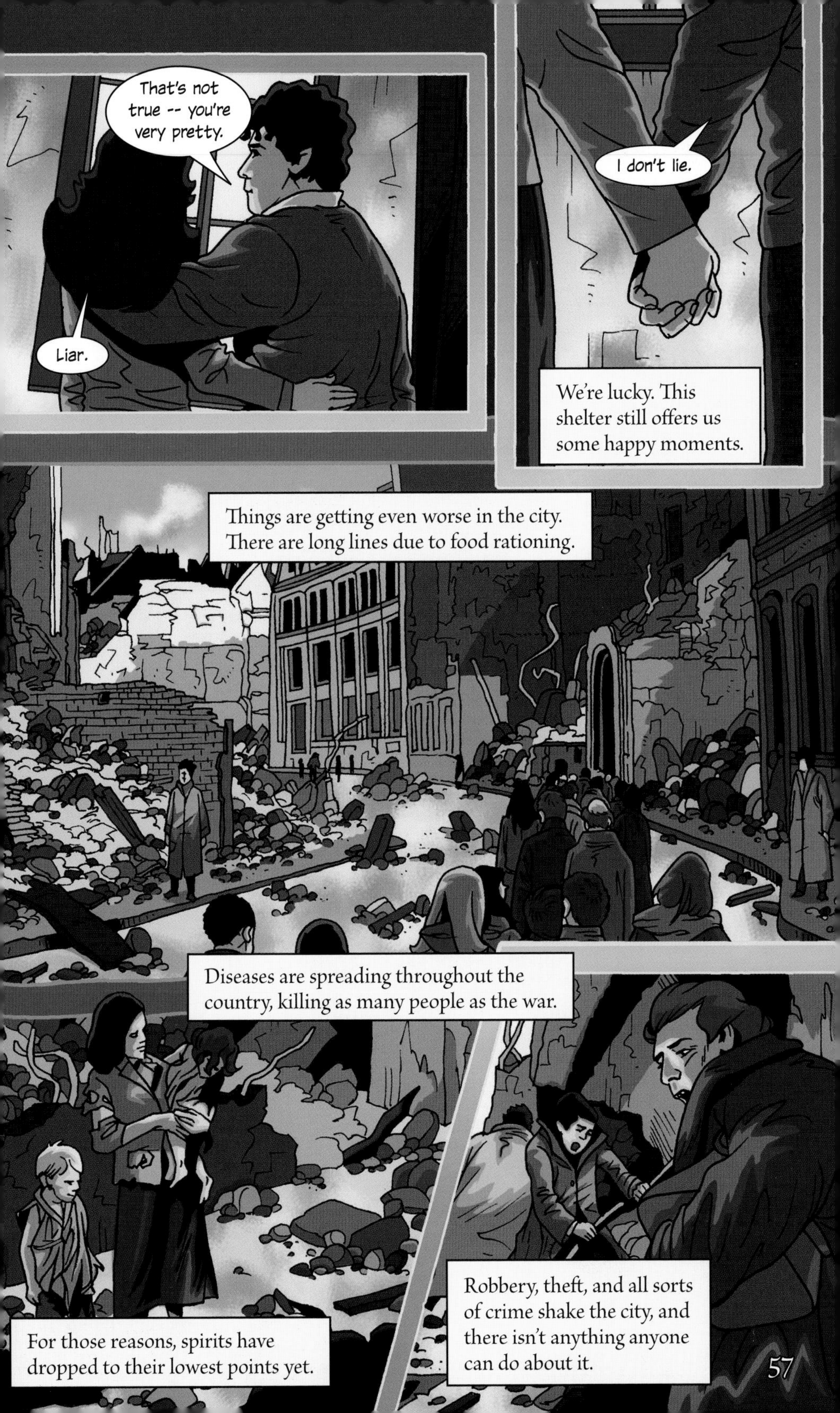
That's not true -- you're very pretty.
Liar.
I don't lie.
We're lucky. This shelter still offers us some happy moments.
Things are getting even worse in the city. There are long lines due to food rationing.
Diseases are spreading throughout the country, killing as many people as the war.
For those reasons, spirits have dropped to their lowest points yet.
Robbery, theft, and all sorts of crime shake the city, and there isn't anything anyone can do about it.

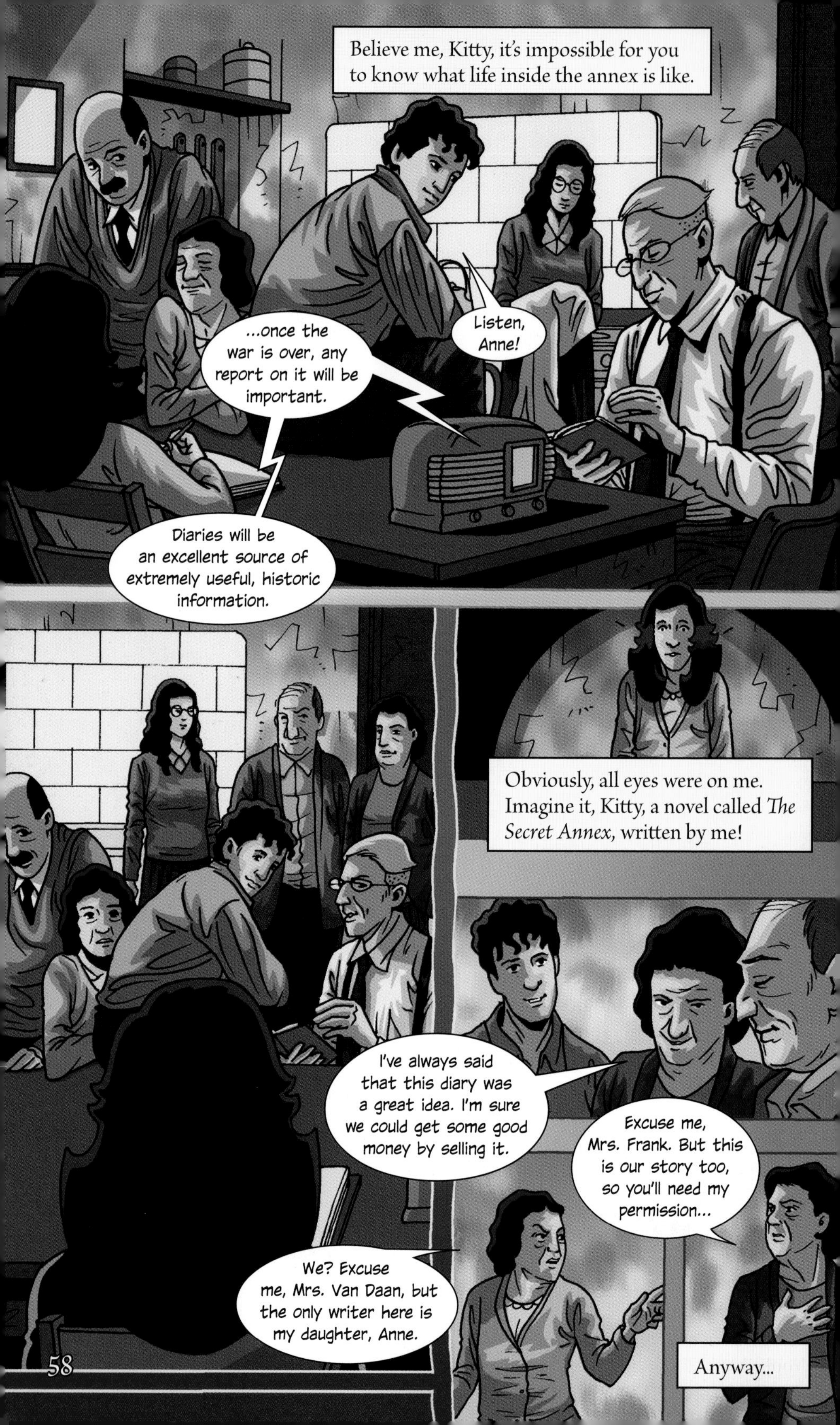
Believe me, Kitty, it's impossible for you to know what life inside the annex is like.
Listen, Anne!
...once the war is over, any report on it will be important.
Diaries will be an excellent source of extremely useful, historic information.
Obviously, all eyes were on me. Imagine it, Kitty, a novel called *The Secret Annex*, written by me!
I've always said that this diary was a great idea. I'm sure we could get some good money by selling it.
Excuse me, Mrs. Frank. But this is our story too, so you'll need my permission...
We? Excuse me, Mrs. Van Daan, but the only writer here is my daughter, Anne.
Anyway...

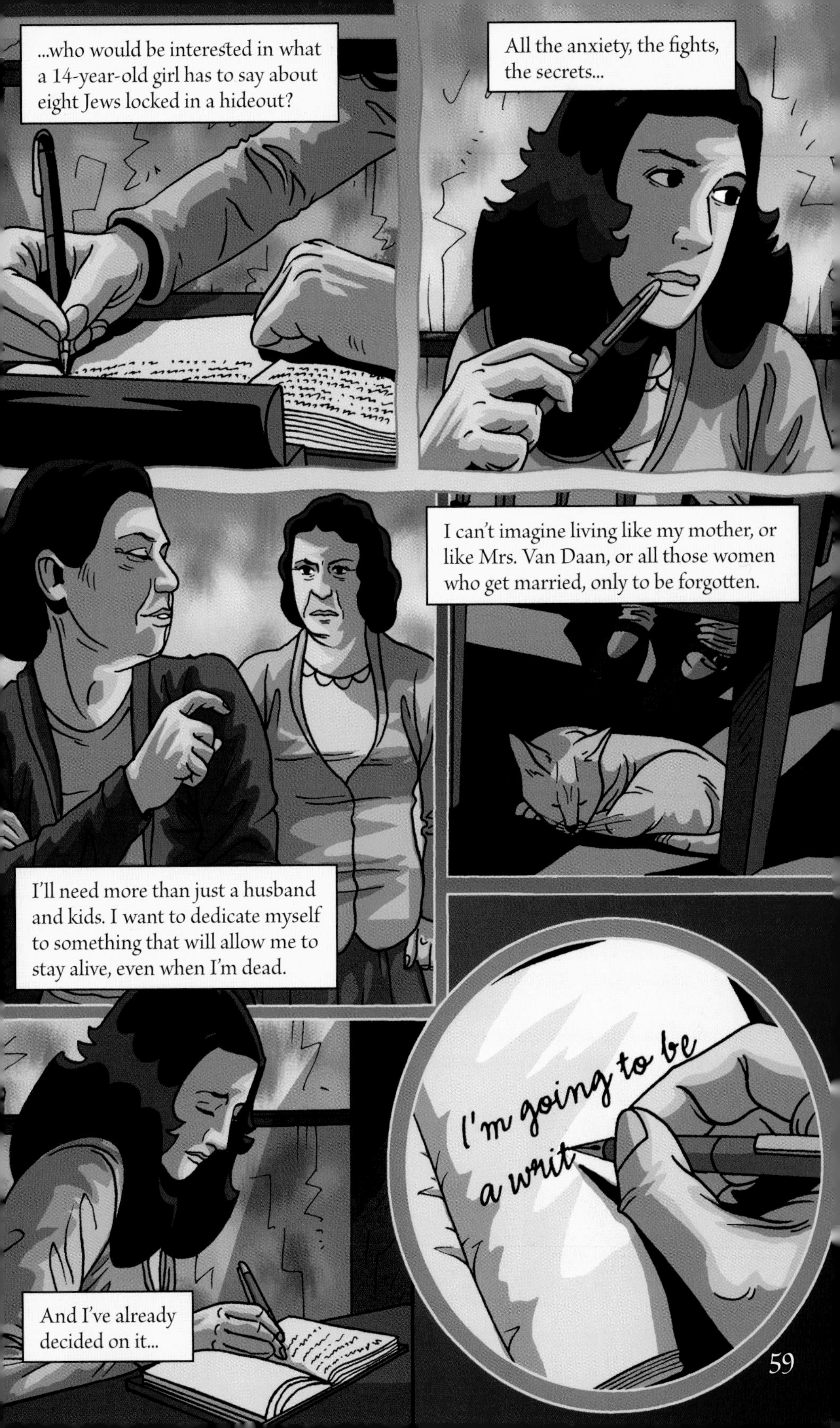
...who would be interested in what a 14-year-old girl has to say about eight Jews locked in a hideout?
All the anxiety, the fights, the secrets...
I can't imagine living like my mother, or like Mrs. Van Daan, or all those women who get married, only to be forgotten.
I'll need more than just a husband and kids. I want to dedicate myself to something that will allow me to stay alive, even when I'm dead.
And I've already decided on it...
I'm going to be a writ

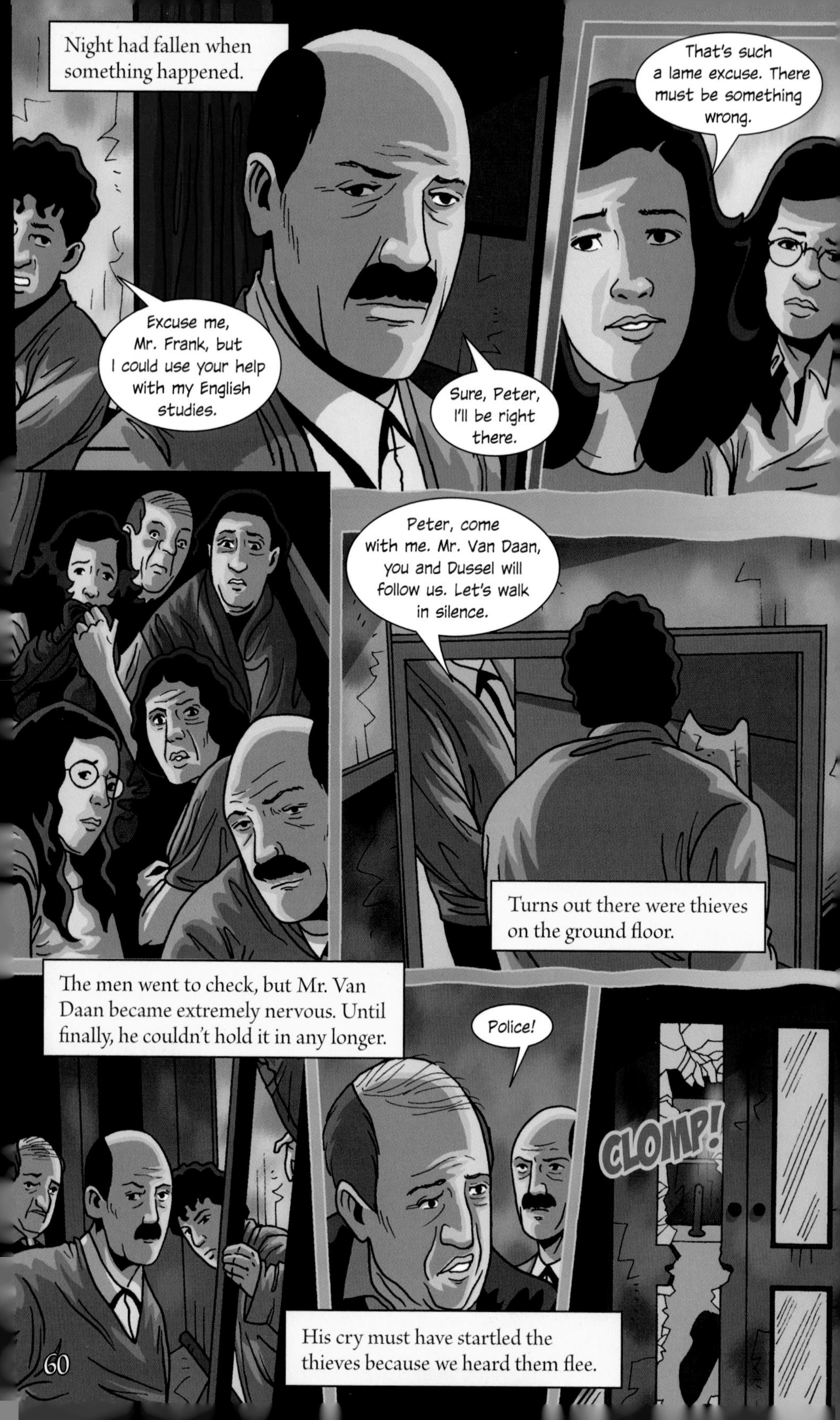
Night had fallen when something happened.
Excuse me, Mr. Frank, but I could use your help with my English studies.
Sure, Peter, I'll be right there.
That's such a lame excuse. There must be something wrong.
Peter, come with me. Mr. Van Daan, you and Dussel will follow us. Let's walk in silence.
Turns out there were thieves on the ground floor.
The men went to check, but Mr. Van Daan became extremely nervous. Until finally, he couldn't hold it in any longer.
Police!
CLOMP!
His cry must have startled the thieves because we heard them flee.

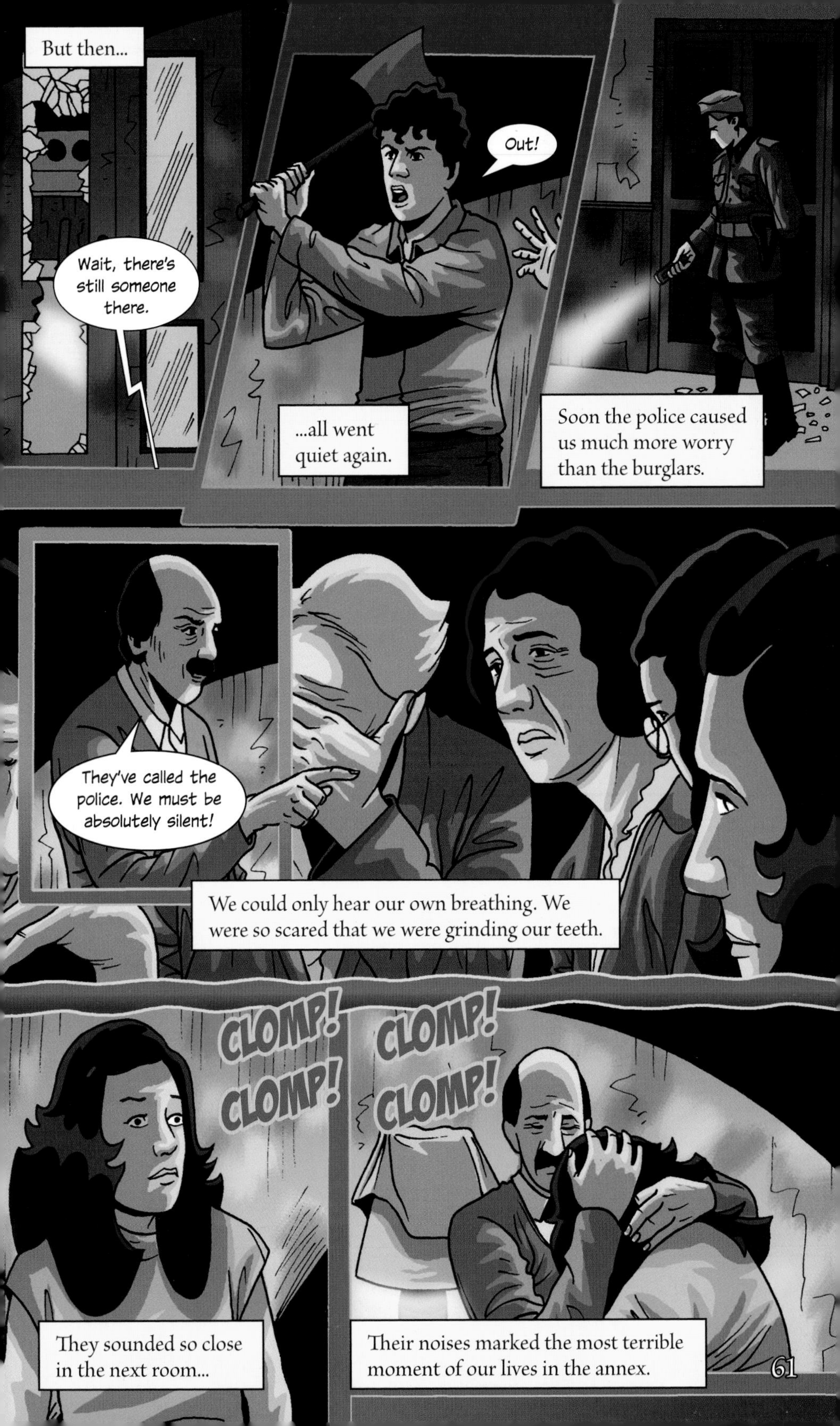
But then...
Wait, there's still someone there.
Out!
...all went quiet again.
Soon the police caused us much more worry than the burglars.
They've called the police. We must be absolutely silent!
We could only hear our own breathing. We were so scared that we were grinding our teeth.
CLOMP! CLOMP!
They sounded so close in the next room...
CLOMP! CLOMP!
Their noises marked the most terrible moment of our lives in the annex.

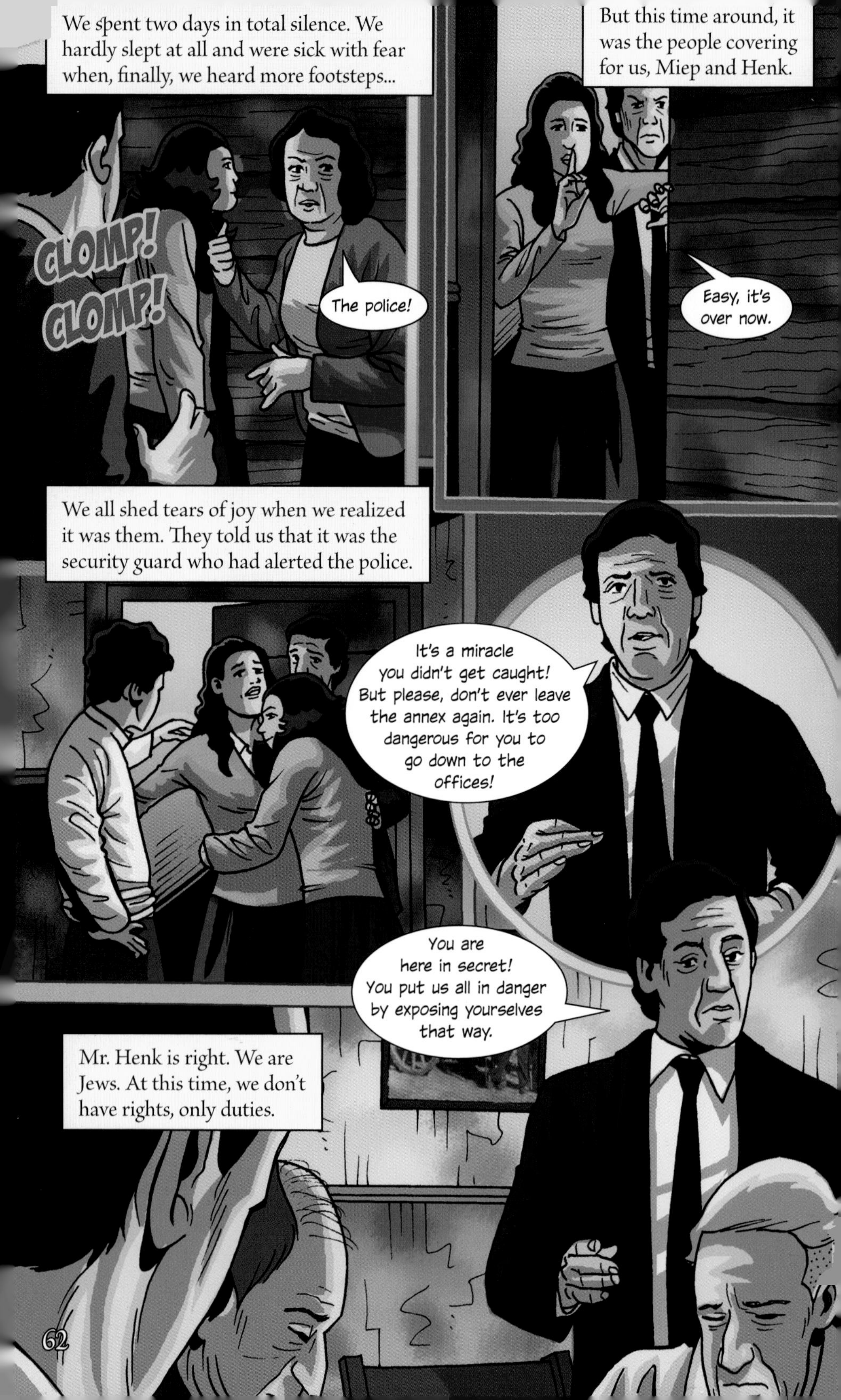
We spent two days in total silence. We hardly slept at all and were sick with fear when, finally, we heard more footsteps...
CLOMP! CLOMP!
The police!
But this time around, it was the people covering for us, Miep and Henk.
Easy, it's over now.
We all shed tears of joy when we realized it was them. They told us that it was the security guard who had alerted the police.
It's a miracle you didn't get caught! But please, don't ever leave the annex again. It's too dangerous for you to go down to the offices!
You are here in secret! You put us all in danger by exposing yourselves that way.
Mr. Henk is right. We are Jews. At this time, we don't have rights, only duties.

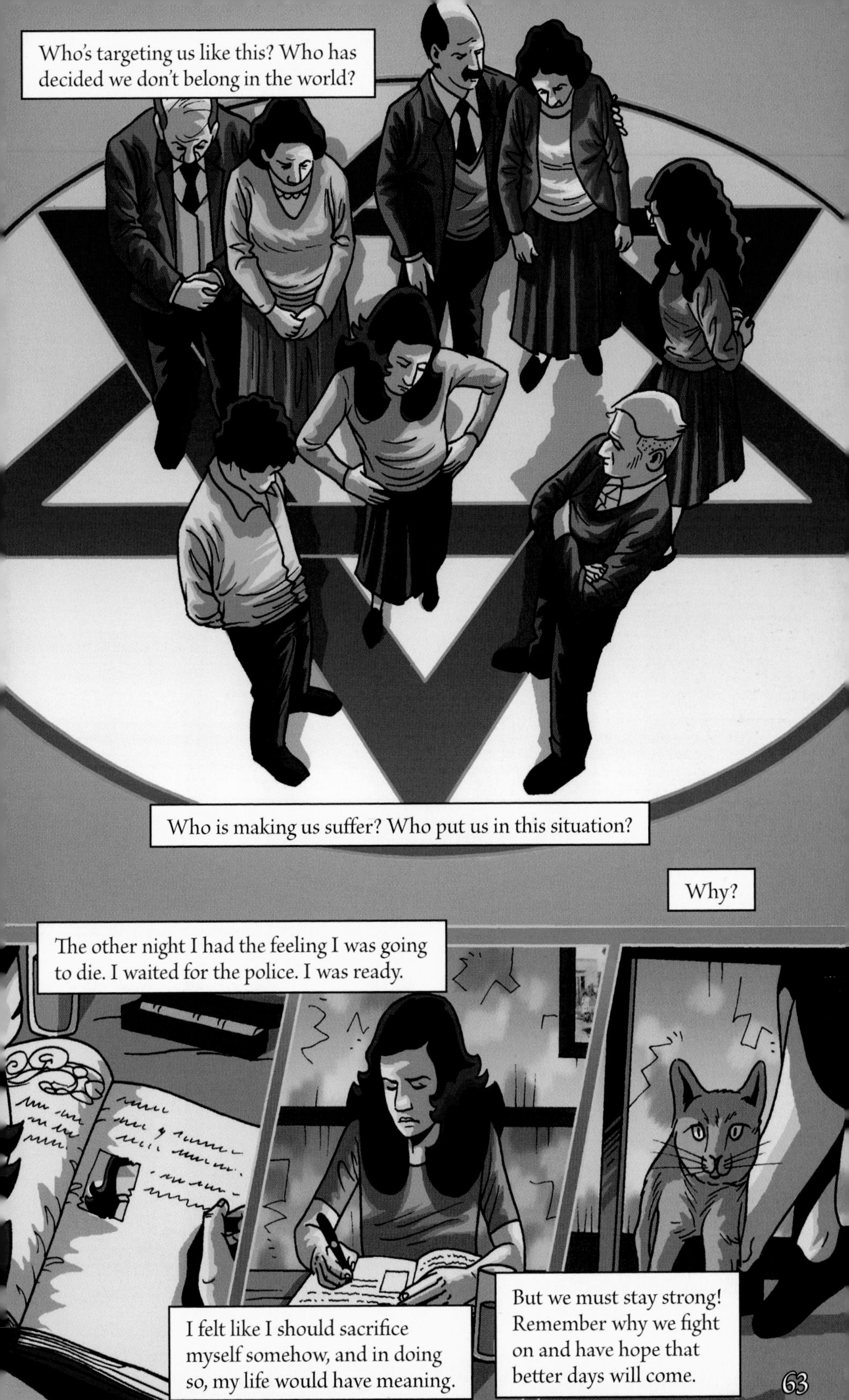
Who's targeting us like this? Who has decided we don't belong in the world?
Who is making us suffer? Who put us in this situation?
Why?
The other night I had the feeling I was going to die. I waited for the police. I was ready.
I felt like I should sacrifice myself somehow, and in doing so, my life would have meaning.
But we must stay strong! Remember why we fight on and have hope that better days will come.

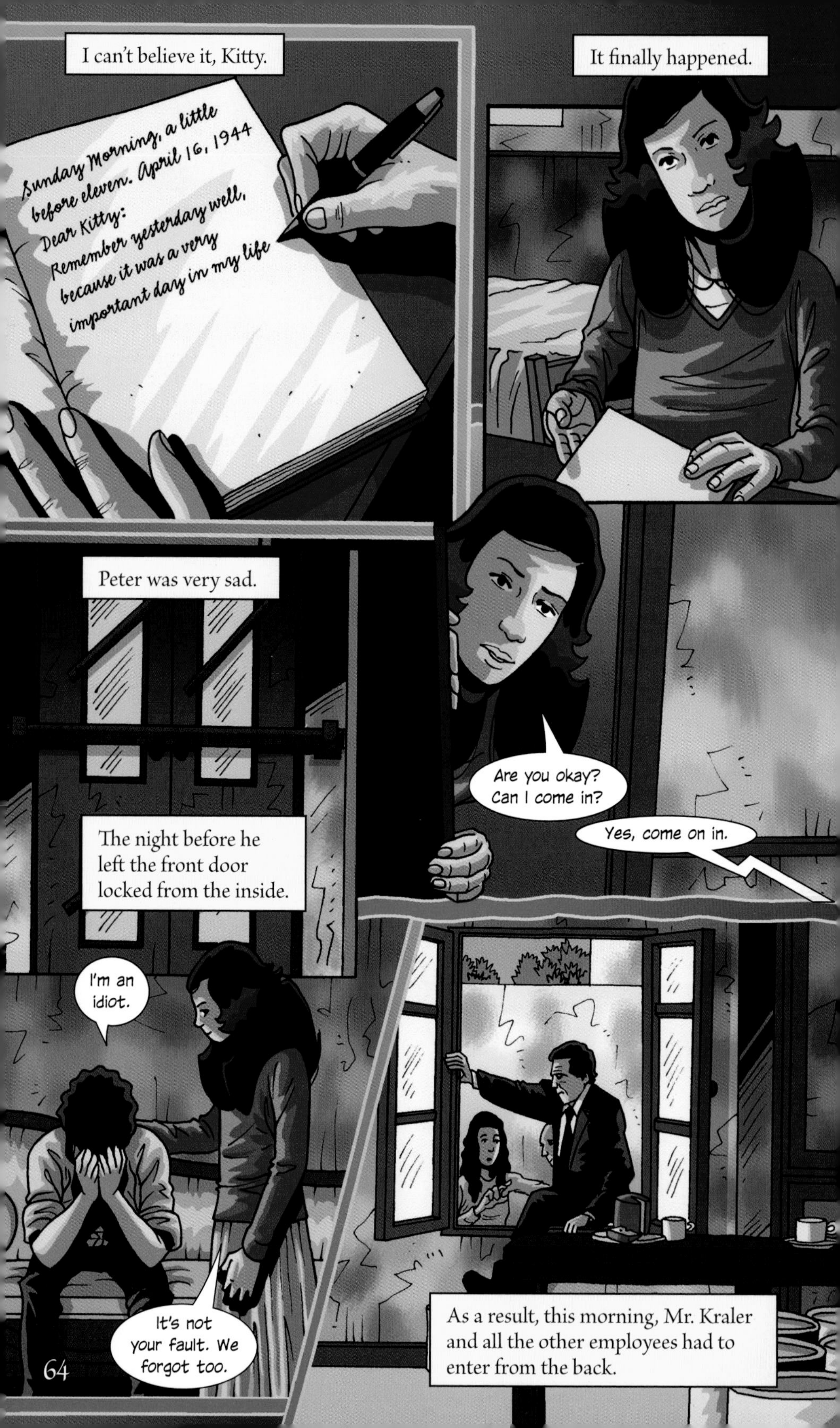
I can't believe it, Kitty.
Sunday Morning, a little before eleven. April 16, 1944
Dear Kitty:
Remember yesterday well, because it was a very important day in my life
It finally happened.
Peter was very sad.
Are you okay? Can I come in?
Yes, come on in.
The night before he left the front door locked from the inside.
I'm an idiot.
It's not your fault. We forgot too.
As a result, this morning, Mr. Kraler and all the other employees had to enter from the back.

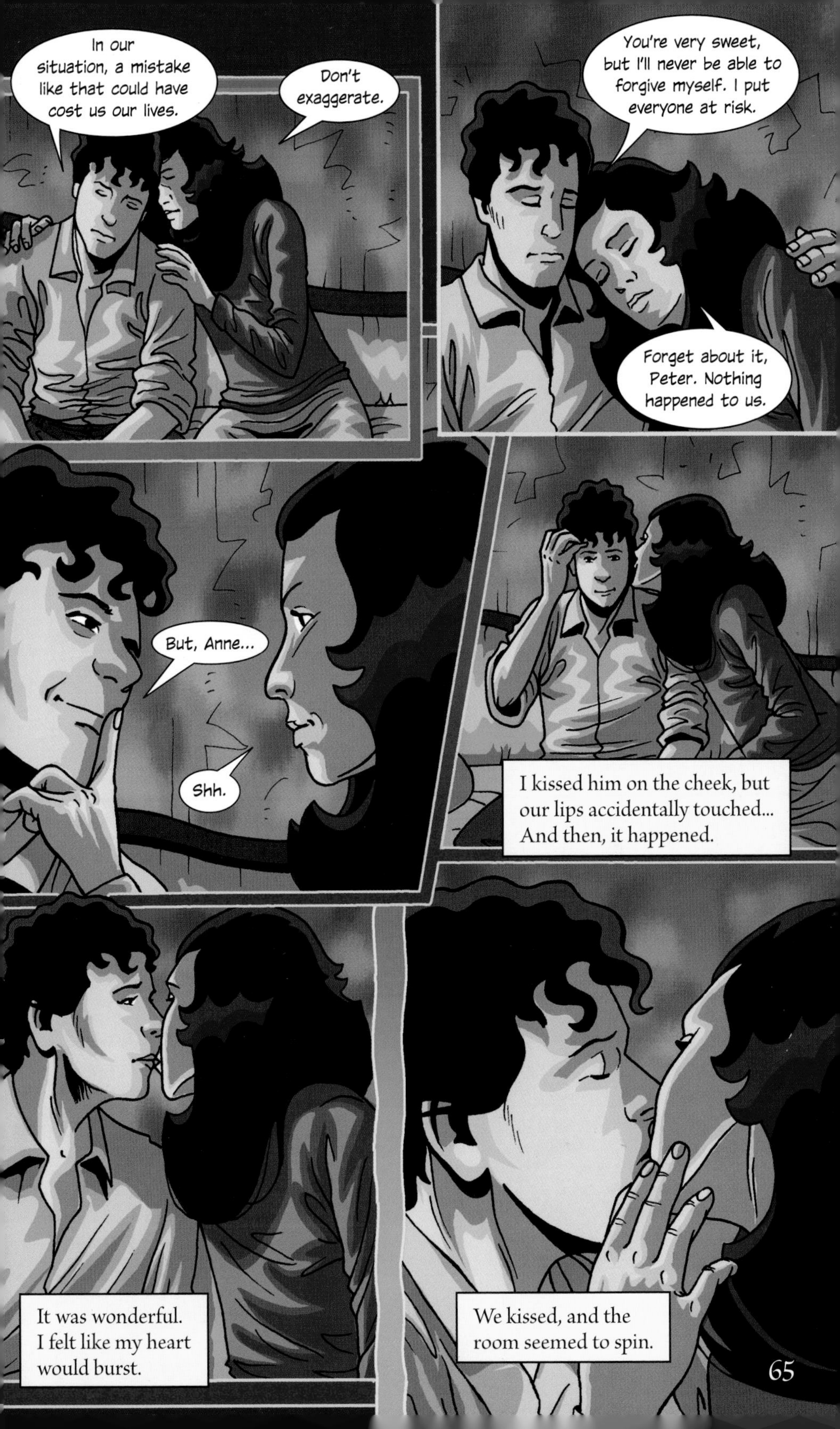

In our situation, a mistake like that could have cost us our lives.
Don't exaggerate.
You're very sweet, but I'll never be able to forgive myself. I put everyone at risk.
Forget about it, Peter. Nothing happened to us.
But, Anne...
Shh.
I kissed him on the cheek, but our lips accidentally touched... And then, it happened.
It was wonderful. I felt like my heart would burst.
We kissed, and the room seemed to spin.

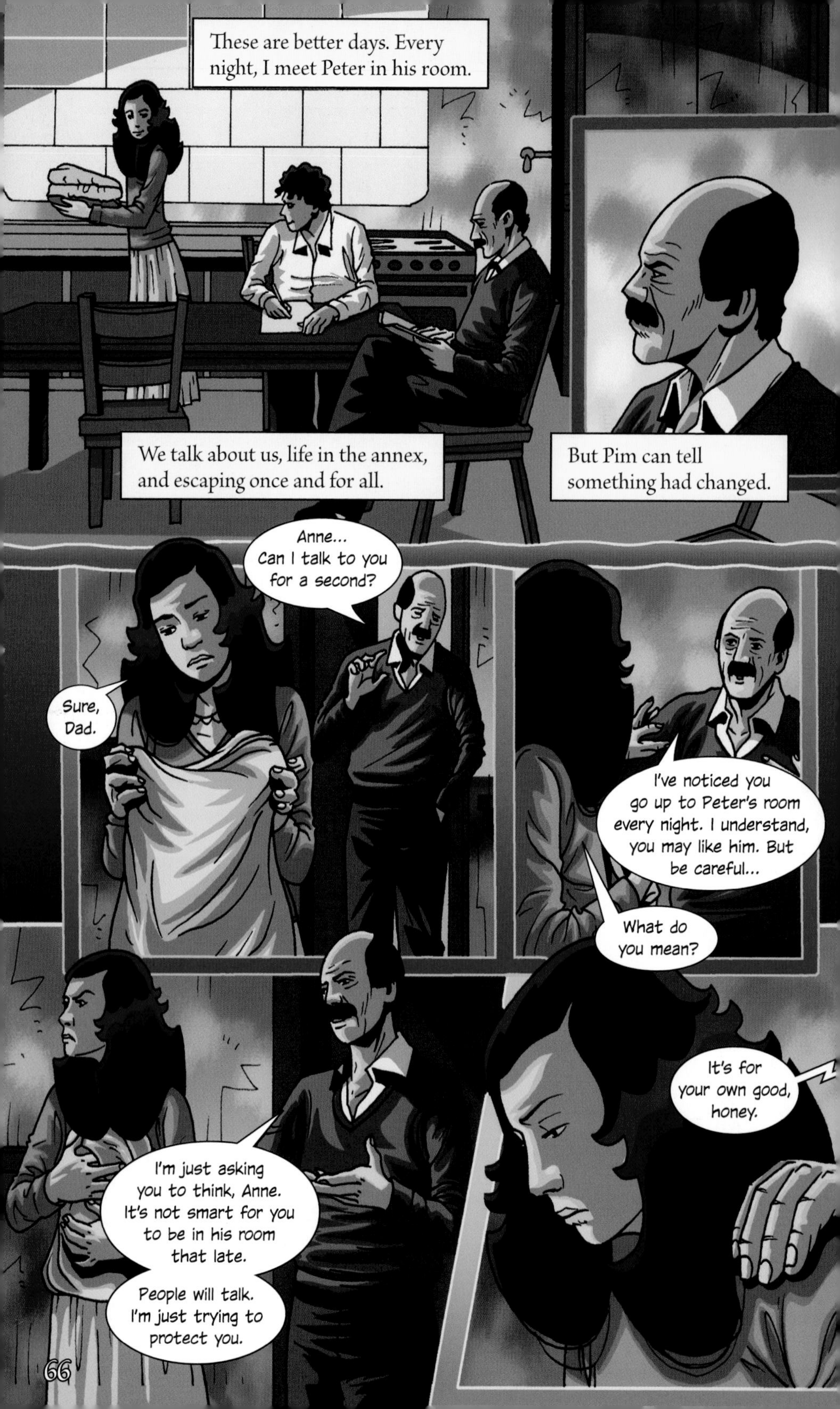
These are better days. Every night, I meet Peter in his room.
We talk about us, life in the annex, and escaping once and for all.
But Pim can tell something had changed.
Anne... Can I talk to you for a second?
Sure, Dad.
I've noticed you go up to Peter's room every night. I understand, you may like him. But be careful...
What do you mean?
I'm just asking you to think, Anne. It's not smart for you to be in his room that late.
People will talk. I'm just trying to protect you.
It's for your own good, honey.

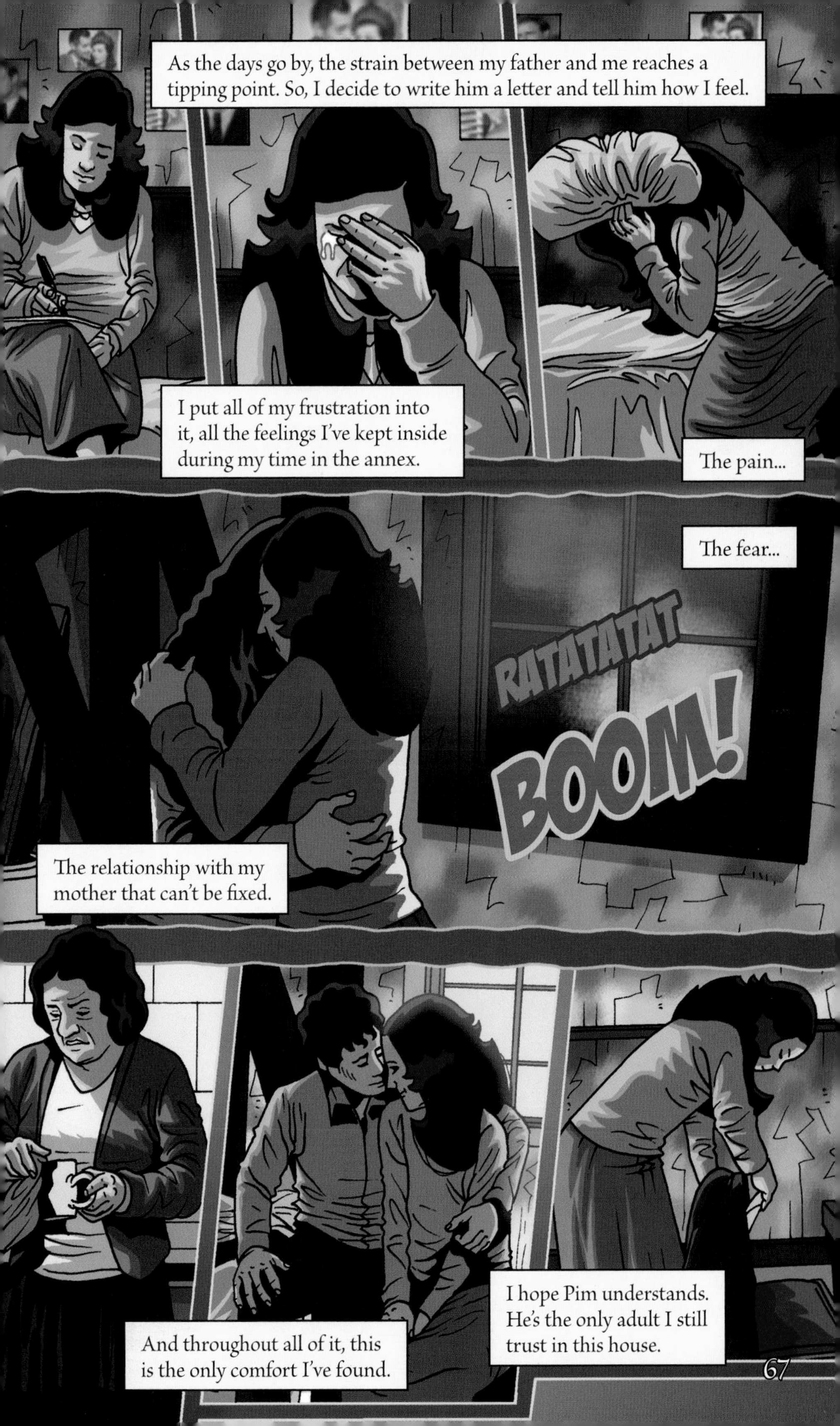
As the days go by, the strain between my father and me reaches a tipping point. So, I decide to write him a letter and tell him how I feel.
I put all of my frustration into it, all the feelings I've kept inside during my time in the annex.
The pain...
The fear...
RATATATAT
BOOM!
The relationship with my mother that can't be fixed.
And throughout all of it, this is the only comfort I've found.
I hope Pim understands. He's the only adult I still trust in this house.

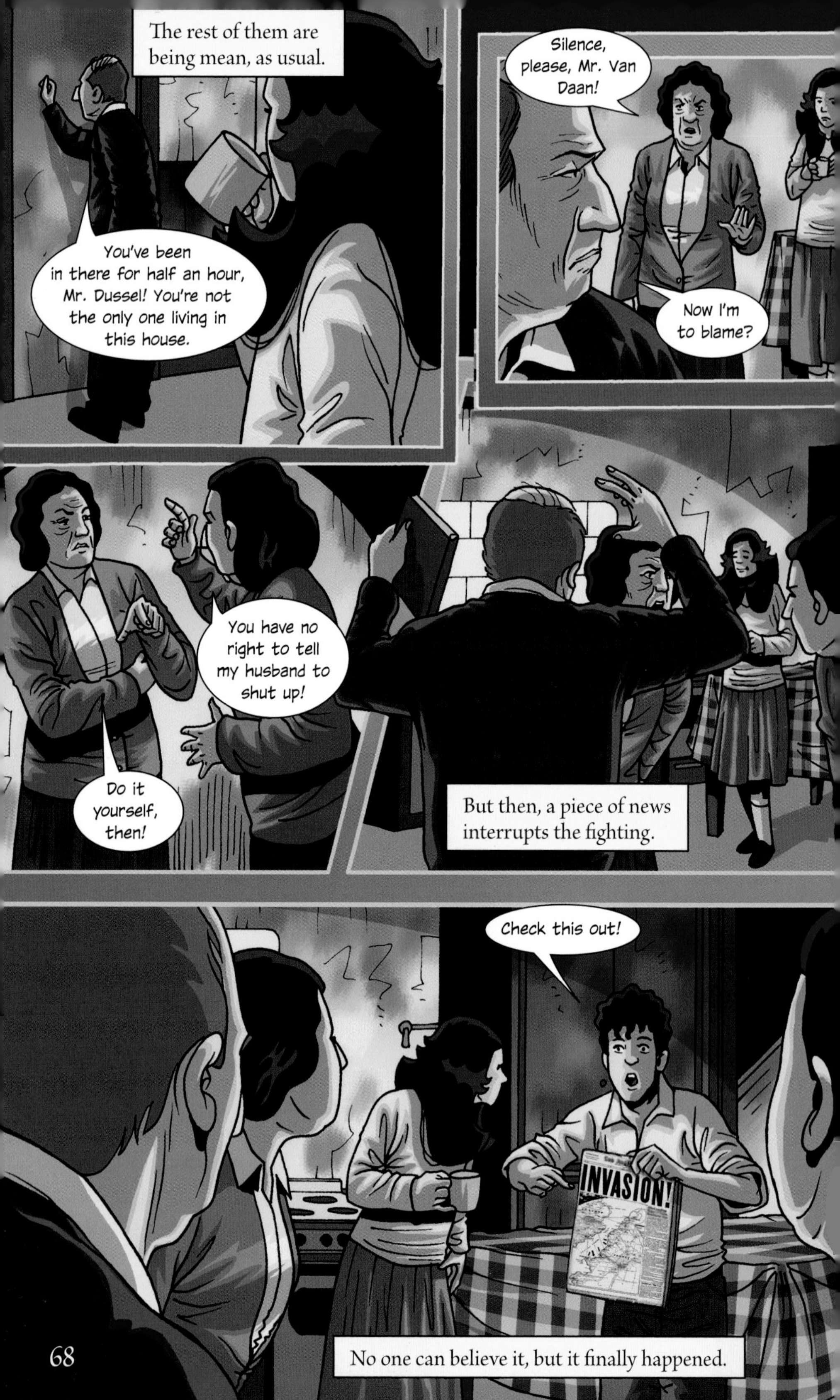
The rest of them are being mean, as usual.
You've been in there for half an hour, Mr. Dussel! You're not the only one living in this house.
Silence, please, Mr. Van Daan!
Now I'm to blame?
You have no right to tell my husband to shut up!
Do it yourself, then!
But then, a piece of news interrupts the fighting.
Check this out!
INVASION!
No one can believe it, but it finally happened.

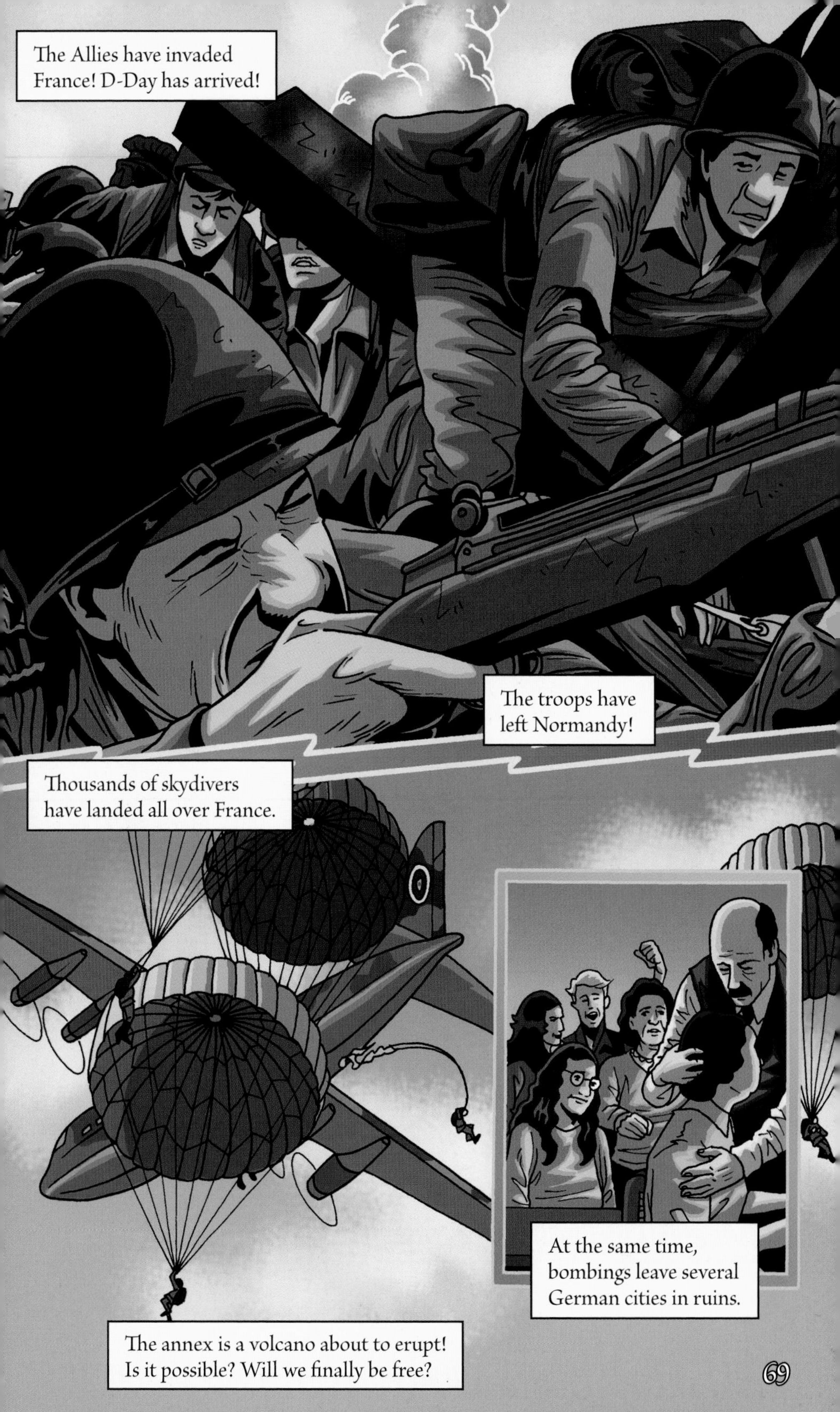
The Allies have invaded France! D-Day has arrived!
The troops have left Normandy!
Thousands of skydivers have landed all over France.
At the same time, bombings leave several German cities in ruins.
The annex is a volcano about to erupt! Is it possible? Will we finally be free?

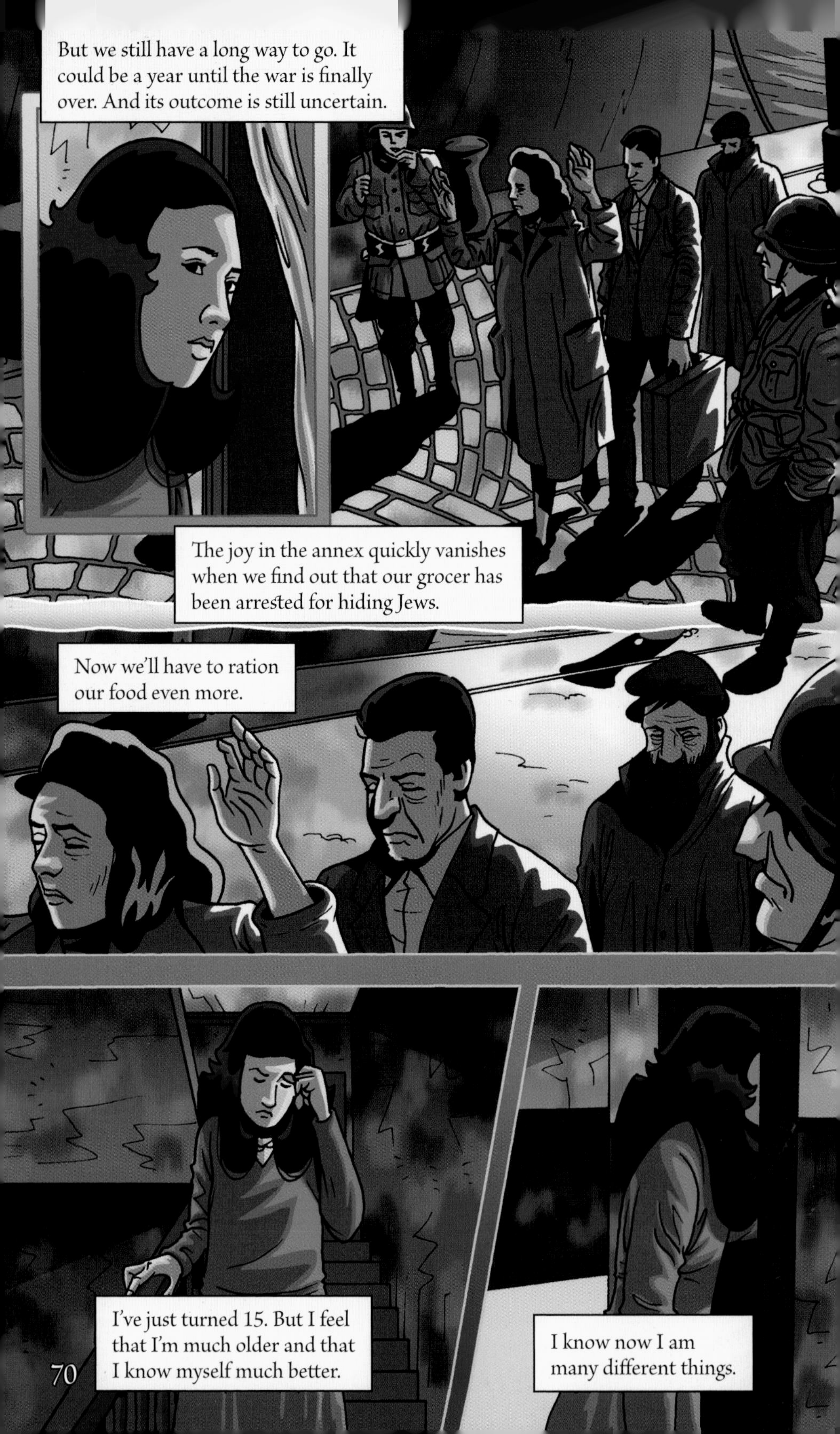
But we still have a long way to go. It could be a year until the war is finally over. And its outcome is still uncertain.
The joy in the annex quickly vanishes when we find out that our grocer has been arrested for hiding Jews.
Now we'll have to ration our food even more.
I've just turned 15. But I feel that I'm much older and that I know myself much better.
I know now I am many different things.

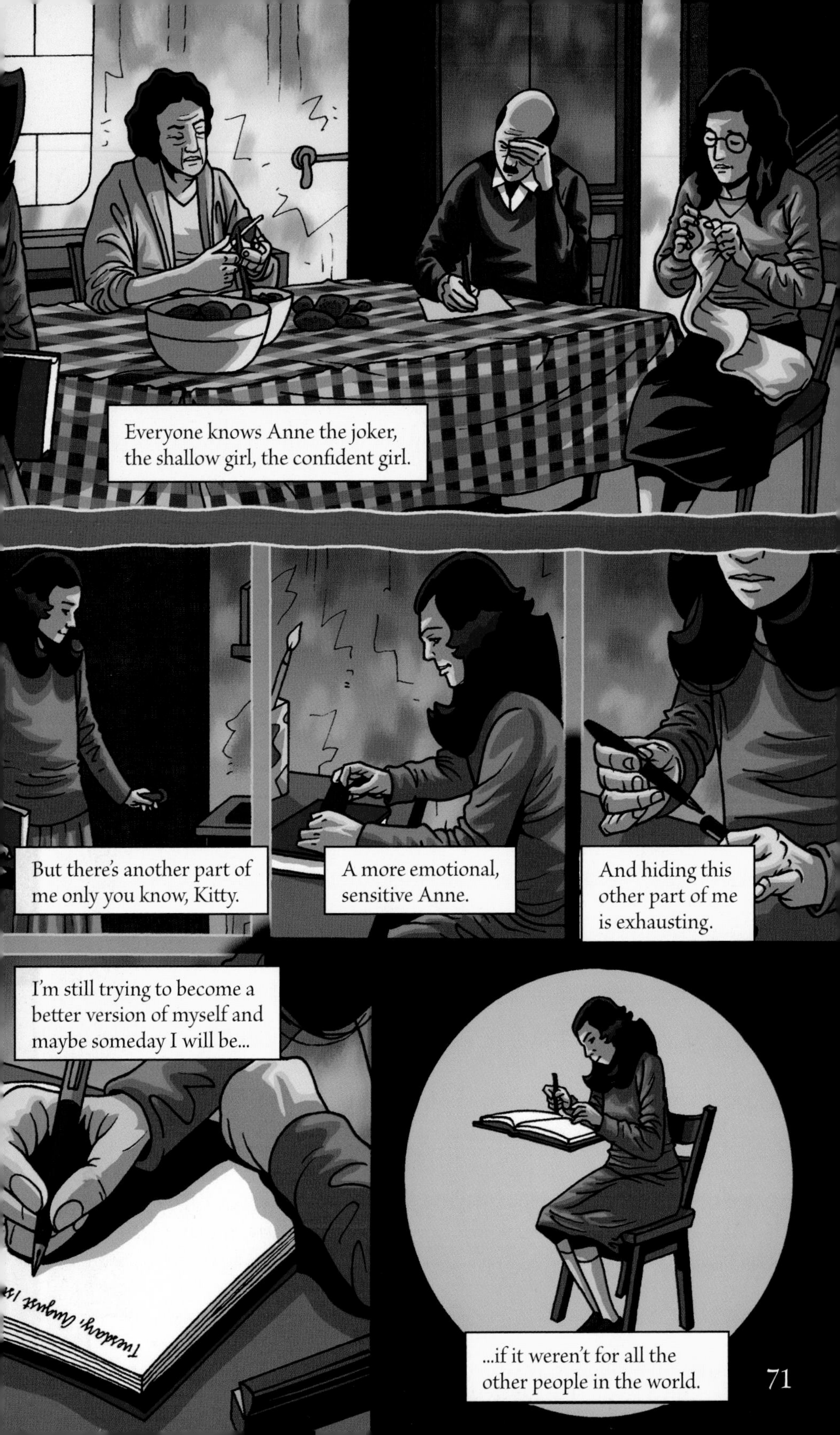
Everyone knows Anne the joker, the shallow girl, the confident girl.
But there's another part of me only you know, Kitty.
A more emotional, sensitive Anne.
And hiding this other part of me is exhausting.
I'm still trying to become a better version of myself and maybe someday I will be...
...if it weren't for all the other people in the world.

ANNE FRANK'S STORY: A LEGACY

When Adolf Hitler, leader of the National Socialist Workers' Party, or the Nazi's, became leader of Germany in 1933, the Frank family could imagine that difficult times would come. This totalitarian party was anti-Semitic, which means it hated Jews. That caused a drastic change in the daily life of all German Jews.

Among other things, the government increasingly restricted the daily lives of Jews, such as assigning specific places for transit or recreation, separate from the rest of the Germans. Jews soon became victims of the Holocaust, the systematic persecution and extermination plan carried out in different concentration camps. This situation continued and worsened during World War II (1939–1945). During the war, Germany occupied several countries, among them Poland and Holland. There, the Nazis captured all Jews. This included the Frank family and their companions, the Van Pels and Mr. Pfeffer (who appear in Anne's diary as the Van Daans and Mr. Dussel), who were discovered in August 1944, after two years of hiding.

In 1945, after the Soviets liberated Auschwitz, one of the cruelest concentration camps, Otto Frank returned to Amsterdam. He soon learned of the death of his entire family. Later, Miep Gies, one of the Franks' loyal protectors while they were in hiding, gave him Anne's diary. It was the only thing left in the house after the arrest. Two years later, Otto fulfilled Anne's wishes and published her diary. It was titled *The Secret Annex*, just as Anne had wished.

After the diary's publication, Otto received and answered many letters from Anne's readers. This work, and his ongoing fight for human rights around the world, continued until his death. The diary became a testament to the Holocaust and was translated into 67 languages.

"The back house," or "the annex," was transformed into a museum thanks to Otto's efforts to preserve and restore it. In 1960, it opened to the public under the name the "Anne Frank House." Today, almost one million people visit it every year. Those who visit can tour the rooms and take part in different activities and workshops. These activities are designed to promote respect for human rights and warn about the dangers of anti-Semitism, racism, and discrimination. In 2010, on the museum's 50th anniversary, Anne's writings were exhibited to the public.

ABOUT ANNE FRANK

Anne Frank was born in 1929 in Frankfurt, Germany. She lived with her parents, Otto and Edith, and her older sister, Margot. With Hitler's rise to power in 1933, they had to leave for Amsterdam. After the beginning of World War II, Holland was invaded by Germany, and the Frank family found itself in danger again. They decided to hide in a secret house behind Otto Frank's office. That same year, Anne received a diary as a birthday gift, a diary she would fill with her experiences and thoughts. In 1944, the residents of the hideout were betrayed by some of their Dutch neighbors and arrested by the Gestapo. They were deported from Holland, and both Anne and her sister were sent to the Bergen-Belsen concentration camp. In March 1945, shortly before the camp was liberated and the war was over, they both died of typhus fever. Otto Frank was the only surviving family member.

ANNE FRANK AND THE MOVIES

In 1959, *The Diary of Anne Frank* made its debut. It was a movie based on a theater play of the same name. Even though the film wasn't a box office hit, it received three Academy Awards, or Oscars. It was one of the first Hollywood movies to tackle the persecution of Jews. Since then, the Holocaust has been featured in more than 20 feature films and documentaries.

Schindler's List was directed by Steven Spielberg in 1993, based on the novel *Schindler's Ark*, by Thomas Keneally. It tells the story of Oskar Schindler, a German businessman who sheltered a thousand Jews in his factory, saving them from the Holocaust. This movie received multiple awards, including seven Oscars.

Life Is Beautiful is a famous 1997 Italian movie set in 1939. It tells the tender yet sad story of the imaginary games that Guido, a Jewish Italian man, makes up so that his son, Giosué, can handle, and finally survive, life in a concentration camp. This movie is based on a book written by an Auschwitz survivor.

In 2002, Roman Polanski brought *The Pianist* to the movie screen. It tells the story of Wladyslaw Szpilman, a Polish pianist and composer who survived both the Warsaw ghetto and World War II. His memoir, *The Pianist: The Extraordinary Story of One Man's Survival in Warsaw, 1939–45*, is one of many horrible tales depicting the Holocaust. In it, Szpilman recounts his life and how he escapes death after being discovered by a German officer. The officer asked him to play a Chopin piece in exchange for letting him live. The movie received many awards, including three Oscars.

GLOSSARY

Allied forces (AL-ide FORSS-ess)—countries united against Germany during World War II, including France, the United States, Canada, Great Britain, and others

annex (AN-eks)—an extra building that is joined onto or placed near a main building

arrogant (A-ruh-guhnt)—exaggerating one's own self-worth or importance, often in an overbearing manner

atmosphere (AT-muhss-fihr)—a mood or feeling of a place

BBC (BBC)—British Broadcasting Corporation; a British public service broadcaster that produces radio and TV shows

chamber pot (CHAYM-buhr POT)—a type of bowl that people used as a toilet

concentration camp (kahn-suhn-TRAY-shuhn KAMP)—a place where thousands of people are held under harsh conditions

confrontational (kuhn-FRUHN-tay-shuhn-uhl)—acting in a threatening way, usually to argue with someone else

defend (di-FEND)—to try to keep someone or something from being harmed

deport (di-PORT)—to send people back to their own country

extermination (ek-STUR-muh-nay-shuhn)—killing or destroying someone or something

gas chamber (GASS CHAYM-buhr)—a room where people are killed with poison gas

Gestapo (guh-STAH-poh)—the secret police of Nazi Germany; the Gestapo is a subdivision of the SS

interrupt (in-tuh-RUHPT)—to get in the way of someone

loyal (LOY-uhl)—being true to something or someone

Nazi (NOT-see)—a member of a political party led by Adolf Hitler; the Nazis ruled Germany from 1933 to 1945

orphan (OR-fuhn)—a child whose parents have died

persecution (PUR-suh-kyoo-shuhn)—cruel or unfair treatment, often because of race or religious beliefs

ration (RASH-uhn)—to limit to prevent running out of something

retired (rih-TIRED)—a person who has given up work usually because of his or her age

socialize (SOH-shuh-lize)—to get together or talk with other people in a friendly way

support (suh-PORT)—to help and encourage someone

tolerant (TOL-ur-uhnt)—able to put up with something

totalitarian (toh-tayl-uh-TEHR-ee-uhn)—of or relating to a political system in which the government has complete control over the people

DISCUSSION QUESTIONS

1. Why do you think Anne Frank's story has touched so many readers?

2. Mrs. Van Daan thinks Anne is a spoiled child. Do you agree? Explain your answer.

3. Do you think you could live a long time locked inside your home? Why or why not?

WRITING PROMPTS

1. Anne Frank described most of her everyday life while she was locked up in the secret annex. What do you think a day in your life would be like if you were locked in your home? What would you do and what wouldn't you do? Write a letter to a friend describing your experience.

2. Anne received her diary when she was thirteen, which helped her realize that she wanted to be a writer. Write a paragraph describing one of your favorite gifts. What makes it so special?

3. Imagine if the Frank family hadn't been arrested and instead was able to leave their hideout in peace. Pretend you're Anne. Write a diary entry about the first thing you would have done once you left the annex.

ABOUT THE AUTHOR

Diego Agrimbau, from Buenos Aires, Argentina, has written more than a dozen graphic novels for various publishing houses around the world. He has won multiple awards, among them the 2005 Prix Utopiales for *Bertold's Bubble*, the 2009 Premio Planeta DeAgostini for Comic Books for *Planet Extra*, and the 2011 Premio Dibujando entre Culturas for *The Desert Robots*. He's currently a contributor to *Fierro* magazine and writes "Los Canillitas" comic scripts for the newspaper *Tiempo Argentino*.

ABOUT THE ILLUSTRATOR

Fabián Mezquita, from Argentina, started publishing his work in 1998. In 2001, he worked for a year as an assistant, and then continued his career as an illustrator, working for ad agencies and various publishing houses, both in Argentina and abroad. He is a founding and active member of Banda Dibujada, a cultural organization created to promote comic books for children and young adults.

READ MORE

Hollingsworth, Tamara. *Anne Frank: A Light in the Dark.* Huntington Beach, Cali.: Teacher Created Materials, 2013.

Hurwitz, Johanna. *Anne Frank: Life in Hiding.* Lincoln, Neb.: University of Nebraska Press, 2014.

Killcoyne, Hope Lourie. *Anne Frank: Heroic Diarist of the Holocaust.* Britannica Beginner Bios. New York: Britannica Educational Publishing, 2016.

INTERNET SITES

Use Facthound to find Internet sites related to this book.

Visit *www.facthound.com*

Just type in 9781515791614 and go!

Check out projects, games and lots more at
www.capstonekids.com

INDEX

Living Philosophies

MAHATMA GANDHI

Illustrations by
ETIENNE
DELESSERT

CREATIVE EDUCATION

Editor: Ann Redpath; Design: Rita Marshall;
Biographical Sketch: Elizabeth Atkinson

Published by Creative Education, Inc., 123 South
Broad Street, Mankato, Minnesota 56001.

Printed in the United States.

Acknowledgement: The writings of Mahatma Gandhi are
used with the permission of Navajivan Trust, Ahmedabad,
India. From *Non-Violence in Peace and War,* by M.K. Gandhi.
From *Mahatma Gandhi's Ideas,* by C.F. Andrew; George Allen
& Unwin (Publishers) LTD.; used by permission of the publisher.

Library of Congress Catalog Card No.: 85-71099
Gandhi, Mahatma; Living Philosophies
Mankato, MN: Creative Education; 32 p.; ISBN: 0-88682-010-3

"Philosophy, if it cannot answer *so many questions as we could wish, has at least the power of* asking *questions which increase the interest of the world and show the strangeness and wonder lying just below the surface even in the commonest things of daily life."*

Bertrand Russell

A living philosophy is something that's alive. It's organic; it has soul.

We *do* philosophy; we don't just *think* about things. And when we *do* philosophy, it becomes more than a class in school, more than thoughts in our heads. It roots itself in our hearts and finds expression in our gestures and actions. It is alive.

All of us ask questions—we've done that since we were young children. Our questions make each of us natural philosophers. But some of us lose that ability to question as we get older. Sometimes we not only forget to ask questions of life, we even begin to live automatically. Yet it's our ability to wonder and ask questions that makes each of us unique (and also makes life more interesting).

Bertrand Russell once wrote: "Philosophy, if it cannot *answer* so many questions as we could wish, has at least the power of *asking* questions which increase the interest of the world and show the strangeness and wonder lying just below the surface even in the commonest things of daily life.'' We wonder, or we philosophize, just as naturally as we breathe. And our own wonderings shape the very life we lead; they become part of our blood and eyesight. Our wonderings define us as individual persons.

Creative's series of living philosophies begins with the thoughts, words and legacies of great thinkers and doers. We read and ponder their philosophies because we can learn from their greatness. But that's not all. A living philosophy—as it's presented here in kernel form—gathers up a whole lifetime of achievement and effort. It gives power and energy and acts like a kernel in us, growing and giving life to our own philosophies. These living philosophies help us find our own motivation, our own source for keeping alive a constant stream of questions about all the life going on around us and in us—beneath every surface.

The Editors
Creative Education

MAHATMA GANDHI ◄

GOur scriptures have laid down certain rules as maxims of human life. The first and foremost is the Vow of Truth.

THE VOW OF TRUTH

Truth—not simply as we ordinarily understand it, not truth which merely answers the saying, "Honesty is the best policy," implying that if it is not the best policy we may depart from it. Here, by Truth we mean that we may have to rule our life by this law of Truth at any cost; and in order to satisfy the definition I have drawn upon the celebrated illustration of the life of Prahlad.

For the sake of Truth Prahlad
dared to oppose his own father;
and he defended himself, not by
paying his father back in his own
coin. Rather in defense of Truth as
he knew it, he was prepared to die
without caring to return the blows
that he had received from his
father, or from those who were
charged with his father's instruc-
tions. Not only that, he would not
in any way even parry the blows;
on the contrary, with a smile on his
lips, he underwent the innumer-
able tortures to which he was subjected, with the result that at last
Truth rose triumphant. Not that he
suffered the tortures because he
knew that some day or other in his
very lifetime he would be able to
demonstrate the infallibility of the
Law of Truth. That fact was there;
but if he had died in the midst of
tortures he would still have
adhered to Truth. That is the Truth
which I would like to follow. In
our Ashram we make it a rule that
we must say "No" when we mean
No, regardless of consequences.

THE DOCTRINE OF AHIMSA

Literally speaking, Ahimsa means "non-killing." But to me it has a world of meaning, and takes me into realms much higher. It really means that you may not offend anybody; you may not harbor an uncharitable thought, even in connection with one who may consider himself to be your enemy. To one who follows this doctrine there is no room for an enemy. But there may be people who consider themselves to be his enemies. So it is held that we may not harbor an evil thought even in connection with such persons.

If we return blow for blow we depart from the doctrine of Ahimsa. But I go farther. If we resent a friend's action, or the so-called enemy's action, we still fall short of this doctrine. But when I say we "resent," I do not say that we should acquiesce: by the word "resenting" I mean wishing that some harm should be done to the enemy; or that he should be put out of the way, not even by any action of ours, but by the action of somebody else, or, say, by divine agency. If we harbor this thought we depart from this doctrine of Non-Violence.

It is an ideal which we have to reach, and it is an ideal to be reached even at this very moment, if we are capable of doing so. But it is not a proposition in Geometry; it is not even like solving difficult problems in higher mathematics—it is infinitely more difficult.

Many of us have burnt the midnight oil in solving those problems. But if you want to follow out this doctrine you will have to do much more than burn the midnight oil. You will have to pass many a sleepless night, and go through many a mental torture, before you can even be within measurable distance of this goal.

A man who believes in the efficacy of this doctrine finds in the ultimate stage, when he is about to

MAHATMA GANDHI

reach the goal, the whole world at his feet. If you express your love in such a manner that it impresses itself indelibly upon your so-called enemy, he must return that love. Under this rule there is no room for organized assassinations, or for murders openly committed, or for any violence for the sake of your country, and even for guarding the honor of precious ones that may be under your charge. After all, that would be a poor defense of their honor.

This doctrine tells us that we may guard the honor of those under our charge by delivering our own lives into the hands of the man who would commit the sacrilege. And that requires far greater courage than delivering blows. If you do not retaliate, but stand your ground between your charge and the opponent, simply receiving the blows without retaliating, what happens? I give you my promise that the whole of his violence will be expended on you, and your friends will be left unscathed.

THE DOCTRINE OF THE SWORD

I do believe that, where there is only a choice between cowardice and violence, I would advise violence. Thus when my eldest son asked me what he should have done, had he been present when I was almost fatally assaulted in 1908, whether he should have run away and seen me killed or whether he should have used physical force which he could and wanted to use, and defended me, I told him that it was his duty to defend me even by using violence. Hence it was that I took part in the Boer War, the so-called Zulu Rebellion and the late war. Hence also do I advocate training in arms for those who believe in the method of violence. I would rather have India resort to arms in order to defend her honour than that she should, in a cowardly manner, become or remain a helpless witness to her own dishonour.

But I believe that non-violence is infinitely superior to violence, forgiveness is more manly than punishment. Forgiveness adorns a soldier. But abstinence is forgiveness only when there is the power to punish; it is meaningless when it pretends to proceed from a helpless creature. A mouse hardly forgives a cat when it allows itself to be torn to pieces by her. But I do not believe India to be helpless. I do not believe myself to be a helpless creature. Only I want to use India's and my strength for a better purpose.

Let me not be misunderstood. Strength does not come from physical capacity. It comes from an indomitable will. An average Zulu is more than a match for an average Englishman in bodily capacity. But he flees from an English boy, because he fears the boy's revolver or those who will use it for him. He fears death and is nerveless in spite of his burly figure.

We in India may realize that one hundred thousand Englishmen

need not frighten three hundred
million human beings. A definite
forgiveness would, therefore,
mean a definite recognition of our
strength. With enlightened forgiveness must come a mighty
wave of strength. It matters little to
me that for the moment I do not
drive my point home. We feel too
downtrodden not to be angry and
revengeful. But I must not refrain
from saying that India can gain
more by waiving the right of punishment. We have better work to
do, a better mission to deliver to
the world.

I am not a visionary. I claim
to be a practical idealist.
The religion of non-
violence is not meant
merely for the saints. It is meant for
the common people as well. Non-
violence is the law of our species as
violence is the law of the brute.
The spirit lies dormant in the
brute, and he knows no law but
that of physical might. The dignity

of man requires obedience to a higher law—to the strength of the spirit.

Non-violence in its dynamic condition means conscious suffering. It does not mean meek submission to the will of the evil-doer, but it means the pitting of one's whole soul against the will of the tyrant. Working under this law of our being, it is possible for a single individual to defy the whole might of an unjust empire to save his honour, his religion, his soul, and lay the foundation for that empire's fall or its regeneration.

My soul refuses to be satisfied so long as it is a helpless witness of a single wrong or a single misery. But it is not possible for me—a weak, frail, miserable being—to mend every wrong or to hold myself free of blame for all the wrong I see. The spirit in me pulls one way, the flesh in me pulls in the opposite direction. There is freedom from the action of these two forces, but that freedom is attainable only by slow and painful stages. I can attain freedom not by a mechanical refusal to act, but only by intelligent action in a detached manner.

Non-violence is not a cover for cowardice, but it is the supreme virtue of the brave. Exercise of non-violence requires far greater bravery than that of swordsmanship. Cowardice is wholly inconsistent with non-violence. Translation from swordsmanship to non-violence is possible and, at times, even an easy stage. Non-violence, therefore, presupposes ability to strike. It is a conscious, deliberate restraint put upon one's desire for vengeance. But vengeance is superior to passive, effeminate and helpless submission.

Forgiveness is higher still.

Vengeance too is weakness. The desire for vengeance comes out of fear of harm, imaginary or real. A dog barks and bites when he fears. A man who fears no one on earth would consider it too troublesome even to summon up anger against one who is vainly trying to injure him. The sun does not wreak vengeance upon little children who throw dust at him. They only harm themselves in the act.

Non-violence is restraint voluntarily undertaken for the good of society. It is, therefore, an intensely active, purifying, inward force. It is often antagonistic to the material good of the non-resister. It may even mean his utter material ruin. It is rooted in internal strength, never weakness. It must be consciously exercised. It therefore presupposes ability to offer physical resistance.

The acquisition of the spirit of non-resistance is a matter of long training in self-denial and appreciation of the hidden forces within ourselves. It changes one's outlook upon life. It puts different values upon things and upsets previous

calculations, and when once it is
intensive enough can overtake the
whole universe. It is the greatest
force because it is the highest
expression of the soul.

All need not possess the same
measure of conscious non-resistance for its full operations. It is
enough for one person only to
possess it, even as one general is
enough to regulate and dispose of
the energy of millions of soldiers
who enlist under his banner, even
though they know not the why
and the wherefore of his
dispositions.

Not to believe in
the possibility of
permanent peace
is to disbelieve in
godliness of human nature.
Methods hitherto adopted have
failed because rock-bottom sincerity on the part of those who
have striven has been lacking. Not
that they have realized this lack.
Peace is unattainable by only part

performance of conditions, even as chemical combination is impossible without complete fulfillment of all the conditions.

If recognized leaders of mankind who have control over engines of destruction were wholly to renounce their use with full knowledge of complications, permanent peace can be obtained. This is clearly impossible without the great powers of the earth renouncing their imperialistic designs. This again seems impossible without these great nations ceasing to believe in soul-destroying competition and to desire to multiply wants and therefore increase their material possessions.

It is my conviction that the root of the evil is want of a living faith in a living God. I have been taught from my childhood, and I have tested the truth by experience, that the meanest of the human species *can* cultivate the primary virtues of mankind. It is this undoubted universal possibility that distinguishes the human from the rest of God's creation. If even one great nation were unconditionally to perform the supreme act of renunciation, many of us would see in our lifetime visible peace established on earth.

Language at best is but a poor vehicle for expressing one's thoughts in full. For me non-violence is not a mere philosophical principle. It is the rule and the breath of my life. I know I fail often, sometimes consciously, more often unconsciously. It is a matter not of the intellect but of the heart. True guidance comes by constant waiting upon God, by utmost humility, self-abnegation, by being ever ready to sacrifice one's self. Its practice requires fearlessness and courage of the highest order. I am painfully aware of my failings.

But the Light within me is steady and clear. There is no escape for any of us save through Truth and non-violence. I know that war is wrong, is an unmitigated evil. I know too that it has got to go. I firmly believe that freedom won through bloodshed or fraud is no freedom. Would that all the acts alleged against me were found to be wholly indefensible rather than that by any act of mine non-violence was held to be compromised or that I was ever thought to be in favour of violence or untruth in any shape or form. Not violence, not untruth, but non-violence, Truth is the law of our being.

The spirit of non-violence necessarily leads to humility. Non-violence means reliance on God, the Rock of Ages. If we would seek His aid, we must approach Him with a humble and a contrite heart. Non-co-operationists may not trade upon their amazing success at the Congress. We must act, even as the mango tree which droops as it bears fruit. Its grandeur lies in its majestic lowliness.

Non-co-operation is not a movement of brag, bluster, or bluff. It is a test of our sincerity. It requires solid and silent self-sacrifice. It challenges our honesty and our capacity for national work. It is a movement that aims at translating ideas into action. And the more we do, the more we find that much more must be done than we had expected. And this thought of our imperfection must make us humble.

When a person claims to be non-violent, he is expected not to be angry with one who has injured him. He will not wish him harm; he will wish him well; he will not swear at him; he will not cause him any physical hurt. He will put up with all the injury to which he is subjected by the wrong-doer. Thus non-violence is complete innocence. Complete non-violence is complete absence of ill-will against all that lives. It therefore embraces even sub-human life, not excluding noxious insects or beasts. They have not been created to feed our destructive propensities. If we only knew the mind of the Creator, we should find their proper place in His creation. Non-violence is therefore in its active form good will towards all life. It is pure Love. I read it in the Hindu scriptures, in the Bible, in the Koran.

Non-violence is a perfect state. It is a goal towards which all mankind moves naturally though unconsciously. Man does not become divine when he personifies innocence in himself. Only then does he become truly man. In our present state, we are partly men and partly beasts and in our ignorance and even arrogance say that we truly fulfill the purpose of our species, when we deliver blow for blow and develop the measure of anger required for the purpose. We pretend to believe that retaliation is the law of our being, whereas in every scripture we find that retaliation is nowhere obligatory but only permissible. It is restraint that is obligatory. Retaliation is indulgence requiring elaborate regulating. Restraint is the law

of our being. For highest perfec-
tion is unattainable without highest
restraint. Suffering is thus the
badge of the human tribe.

The goal ever recedes from us.
The greater the progress, the
greater the recognition of our
unworthiness. Satisfaction lies in
the effort, not in the attainment.
Full effort is full victory.

FASTING

If the struggle which we are
seeking to avoid with all our might
has to come, and if it is to remain
non-violent as it must in order to
succeed, fasting is likely to play an
important part in it. It has its place
in the tussle with authority and
with our own people in the event
of wanton acts of violence and
obstinate riots, for instance.

There is a natural prejudice
against it as part of a political
struggle. It has a recognized place
in religious practice. But it is considered a vulgar interpolation in
politics by the ordinary politician
though it has always been resorted
to by prisoners in a haphazard way
with more or less success. By

fasting, however, they have always succeeded in drawing public attention and disturbing the peace of jail authorities.

To practice non-violence in mundane matters is to know its true value. It is to bring heaven upon earth. There is no such thing as the other world. All worlds are one. There is no 'here' and no 'there'. The whole universe including the most distant stars, invisible even through the most powerful telescope in the world, is compressed in an atom. I hold it therefore to be wrong to limit the use of non-violence to cave dwellers and for acquiring merit for a favoured position in the other world. All virtue ceases to have use if it serves no purpose in every walk of life. I would therefore plead with the purely political-minded people to study non-violence and fasting as its extreme manifestation with sympathy and understanding.

MAHATMA GANDHI

*Generations to come, it may be,
will scarce believe that such a one
as this ever in flesh and blood
walked upon this earth.*

Albert Einstein

MAHATMA GANDHI

Mohandas Karamchund Gandhi, more often
referred to as "Mahatma" or the "great soul,"
dedicated his life to the independence of
India and strived for equality among his
people. In the process, he emerged as an
international symbol and model
humanitarian.

Born into the Bania caste on October 2,
1869 in Gujarat, West India, Gandhi led a
comfortable life as the son of a well-
respected government official. His philosophical and moral convictions were shaped
at an early age by his mother who remained
a very devout Hindu of the Vaisnavism sect.
Gandhi was considered to be an average stu-
dent at school, and at home he was coopera-
tive and generous.

Gandhi married at age thirteen, as is the
custom of India, through an arrangement
made by his parents. (This later prompted
him to speak out against child marriages.)
After experiencing an adolescent rebellious
stage, he devoted himself entirely to self-
improvement and to the religious system
with which he was raised.

After much debate Gandhi left for London
to study law. The adjustment to western
urban life was difficult, but he found support
through his committment to vegetarianism
and his interest in the moral and societal
problems of England. In 1891 he returned to

India, only to discover that his mother had died and that his prospects of a legal career were limited.

Gandhi eventually accepted a contract from an Indian law firm in Natal, South Africa, after holding several unsuccessful jobs at home. His experiences of discrimination in Africa presented challenges to him. Here he faced the moment of truth. He realized that his emotional outbursts following displays of discrimination were counter-productive personally, as well as professionally. He needed to find dignity as an Indian and as a human being.

Following the Boer War, Gandhi decided that he had made little real impact in South Africa, even though his work for Indian rights had brought him worldwide attention. However he did return to India with new insights; he believed that all religions were true and all people must be treated equally. In Africa he also learned the great power of mass civil disobedience, rooted in Satygraha or ''firmness in truth.''

His increasing involvement in politics and the Amritsar Massacre (1919), in which nearly 400 Indians were slain, prompted Gandhi into leading his people to full independence from Britain. He never put blame on the British for the political situation, but instead he concentrated on strengthening Indian nationalism. He lead non-violent protests and accepted punishment of imprisonment cooperatively, quietly. His most notable demonstrations involved the march against the salt tax and the boycott of foreign goods for the purpose of encouraging cottage industry and self-sufficiency.

Over a period of several years Gandhi organized talks with Britain and represented India at conferences. His popularity and influence fluctuated politically during this time, but his philosophy of non-violence and self-improvement continued to inspire people of all nations. On August 17, 1947, India finally attained independence.

In January of 1948, Mohandas Gandhi was murdered on his way to evening prayers by a fanatical Hindu. The entire world, together, mourned their loss of this great soul. His message shall remain timeless. "Truth will endure, all the rest will be swept away before the tide of time."

"I wanted to draw these great faces to be like sculpture," Etienne Delessert said. "I wanted them to be graphic but passionate—as the people themselves were. I don't think Gandhi should always be presented as overly serious. Certainly he cried and laughed as every person does."

Etienne Delessert, born in 1941 in Lausanne, Switzerland, is a painter, graphic designer, film producer, illustrator, editor, and publisher of children's books—in other words, a Renaissance man.

Delessert has lived most of his life with the exquisite Swiss landscape always on his horizon, yet his artwork shows a universal landscape. His has the view of a world citizen.

His awards are many. He won the Bologna International Grand Prize for his *Yok-Yok* series, Best European Book Award, and honor prize in the Hans Christian Andersen Award of 1980. He has had a one-man show at Le Musèe des Arts Decoratiff du Louvre in Paris.

He divides his work among three locations: Lausanne, Paris, and New York, collaborating with various European and American publishers.